Towards an open school

The man who never alters his opinion is like
standing water and breeds reptiles of the mind.

William Blake

Towards an open school

A commentary on innovations and directions
in post-primary teaching

John Watts
Principal, Countesthorpe College

Longman

LONGMAN GROUP LIMITED
London
Associated companies, branches and representatives
throughout the world

© Longman Group Limited 1980

First published 1980
ISBN 0 582 36311 X
0036917
Printed in Hong Kong by
Wilture Enterprises (International) Ltd.

This book is dedicated to my grandchildren, Ben and Emma, and all 'the sons and daughters of Life's longing for itself'.

Contents

Preface

Five years ago I wrote a book about teaching (*Teaching*, published 1974 by David and Charles). In it, I tried to give a picture of what it is like to be a schoolteacher, describing what I knew to be there in the schools. Although my own principles must have been apparent in the book, I found myself, when writing it, constantly stopping short of speculation about alternatives, of projections of what might happen in future schools, or, taking the moral bull by the horns, of what I thought schools *ought* to be like. Perhaps I felt also that 'next year's words await another voice'.

After five years, my convictions of what school should be like have grown no weaker, and yet I cannot often agree with the other voices nowadays. The trend has been towards an assertion that education is a matter of telling the young what other people have decided they ought to know. The effect of this assertion has been to make teachers revert to instruction in what have been thought of as the basic skills. I happen to favour proficiency in basic skills, though in this book I argue for a list of survival skills that extends a lot further than, while not excluding, the traditional three Rs. What I fear, and identify in too many instances, is the reduction of education to a joyless drilling that is concerned primarily to rehearse the young for a joyless life in adult society. Education should not be a rehearsal, but a celebration of Life. As parents and teachers, we should be finding out how to mount that celebration, not be conditioning our children to accept Life as a strait-jacket.

I am not sure whether this sounds *avant-garde* or quaintly old-fashioned, and I don't very much mind. What I am convinced about is the quality of living that my children and grandchildren can hope to enjoy. This is only in part a question of what material prosperity they may achieve: it has more to do with their capacity to know themselves, collaborate in peace with their neighbours and find fulfilment by doing whatever they are best at.

I am also convinced after twenty-five years of teaching (and I am still for most of my time a teacher) that radical changes in schooling are not only urgently necessary but that means can be found to bring them about. I am surer than ever that changes in school are eventually inescapable: the issue is one of whether those changes will be superficial, responding only to the appearance of trends, or whether they will be radical, determined by clear aims and shorter-term objectives. It is also an issue of whether the changes are to be imposed upon us by forces and bodies outside the reach of the users of the schools, or whether by taking fate into our own hands, these changes may be shaped by those of us whom they most affect, namely the students, parents and teachers.

This book is therefore addressed to those who *use* schools, not to those with an armchair or lecture-room interest, but to those who are committing their lives or their children's lives to our schools.

One of my occupations is bee-keeping. I often relax by watching these busy creatures making their way in and out of their hives, and I try to fathom the mystery of their instinctive and self-sacrificing dedication to the spirit of the hive. My critics have suggested that my interest reflects a suppressed desire to dominate and regiment others towards orderly productivity. They could not be further from the truth, for I regard these insects as a dreadful warning of what society or school could become once the individual is lost sight of, and all is sacrificed to mindless obedience and industry. Long may I relieve my bees of their surplus honey, while their perfectly structured society reminds me that education must remain firmly rooted in human diversity and unpredictability. Let the hive remain closed and the school become open.

John Watts
Countesthorpe, May 1978

1 The good old days?

Why should schools change at all? Why can't they stay as they are? Or to put the question in its more usual form – Why weren't they left as they were? It is never quite clear when the golden age of schools was exactly, but at some time, it seems, within living memory even, there was a peak in the level of public education since when all has been decline and decay. Or so we keep hearing. Once upon a time, they could all read and write, recite their tables and work out in their heads how many men were needed to dig a ditch half a mile long in half a day.

But, alas, it is a fairy story. Even in the years between the wars, before tractors had ditching attachments, and gangs of navvies whose literacy nobody needed to worry about really were digging trenches, the record being laid down was nowhere near as rosy. For every boy who knew who Titus Oates was, and every girl who could tell Debussy from Verdi,[1] there were whole battalions who left school resenting it all as a wasted time of pointless drudgery and servitude.

'I looked forward to leaving school so that I could get educated', as one shrewd countryman put it, looking back to the start of the century.[2]

Gerard Holmes gave a picture of Lancashire elementary schooling just after the First World War:

> There followed a distribution of this crowd of automata into classrooms, sixty or more into each, where they were jammed together into rows of long desks and fed with standardised information and trained and tested in memorising.
>
> Here life was simplified by obedience to orders: 'all stand', 'all sit', 'sit straight', 'pencils up', 'pencils down', 'open books', 'close books', 'pass books', are such as may remind many of the happiest days of their lives.

Lest some child might be actually starving for information and might become engrossed in the subject that was being spoon-fed to the class, the teaching was deliberately interrupted every thirty-five or forty minutes throughout the nine or so years the child spent at school, by the ringing of a bell or other means, and a shift of interest compelled. Thus was secured a complete inability to concentrate on anyone's part, teacher's or child's.[3]

More recently, in 1963, Sir John Newsom, commissioned by the government to enquire into the education of the average child, found widespread shortcomings and dissatisfaction, a disregard for 'half our future'.[4] Were standards dropping already? It would seem there was precious little distance for them to drop. After the First World War, concern about attainment levels led to a government enquiry and the Newbolt Report of 1921.[5] Its gloomy picture includes a familiar comment from employers when asked about school-leavers: 'All complained, often bitterly, of defects in spelling, punctuation, vocabulary, and sentence structure. Spelling, in particular, received adverse comment.'

The Spens Report[6] of 1938 found little difference and by the time of the Second World War, the Norwood Report of 1943 concluded that 'the evidence is such as to leave no doubt in our minds that we are here confronted with a serious failure of the secondary schools... too many pupils show marked inability to present ideas clearly to themselves, to arrange them and to express them clearly on paper or in speech'.[7]

Was the golden age then a little further back? A hundred years ago the picture seems very little different. Here is a recollection of schooling in Warwickshire in about 1870.

Right up the school, through all the six standards (there was a special class of a few boys and one or two girls above this) you did almost nothing except reading, writing and arithmetic. What a noise there used to be! Several children would be reading aloud, teachers scolding, infants reciting, all waxing louder and louder until the master rang the bell on his desk and the noise slid down to a lower note and less volume.

Reading was worst; sums you did at least write on your slate, whereas you might wait the whole half-hour of a reading lesson while boys and girls who could not read stuck at every word. If you took your finger from the word that was being read you were punished by staying in when others went home. A specially hard time was the two 'sewing afternoons'. While the girls were collected together for sewing, the boys merely did more sums or an extra dictation, just the sort of thing they had been doing all morning. As they craned their necks to see what sort of garments, what colours, were coming out of the vicarage basket of mending, they were unusually tiresome to the poor pupil-teacher, losing their places over and over again, or misspelling words they knew perfectly well – forgetting everything. He rapped with a stick; he shouted; he called out, 'Jack, Tom, stay in half an hour!' – a rather effective threat. To remain in school was the thing above all others the children did not want to do.

'How dull school was!' my father summed up. And yet – no, not dull. One didn't learn much but the place was full of feeling. It was so easy to get a beating for one thing. Some boys couldn't get through a day without 'holding out their hands' or a week without a real thrashing. While a thrashing proceeded the school simmered. Would a boy cry out? Was the master hitting harder than usual? It might be oneself soon.

Two inspectors came once a year and carried out a dramatic examination. The schoolmaster came into school in his best suit; all the pupils and teachers would be listening till at ten o'clock a dog-cart would be heard on the road, even though it was eighty yards away. In would come two gentlemen with a deportment of high authority, with rich voices. Each would sit at a desk and children would be called in turn to one or other. The master hovered round, calling children out as they were needed. The children could see him start with vexation as a good pupil stuck at a word in the reading-book he had been using all the year, or sat motionless with his sum in front of him. The master's anxiety was deep, for his earnings depended on the children's work. One year the atmosphere of anxiety so affected the lower standards that, one after another as they were brought to the Inspector, the boys howled and the girls whimpered. It took hours to get through them. But the older children looked beyond the examination; the moment the Inspectors had finished the school would be closed. Well, not quite at that moment; time would be taken to open a hamper of great, golden, rare fruit, of which each child would presently have a specimen cupped in his own two hands – oranges![8]

It would take a good many oranges to recompense that sort of educational injustice. The man who recollected those days, Joseph Ashby, transcended his privations to embark upon a lifetime of self-education. The more is the wonder since the system was designed not to bring enlightenment to the benighted, but, in the words of a leading educational reformer of the time, for 'the rearing of hardy, intelligent working men, whose character and habits shall afford the greatest amount of security to the property and order of the community...it is chiefly intended that the practical lesson, that they are destined to earn their livelihood by the sweat of their brow shall be inculcated'.[9]

So much for the children of the labouring class 100 years ago. How about contrasting a bright boy in a European school a little nearer the end of the century. Is he very far removed from Gerard Holmes's Lancashire children 'fed with standardised information'? Here is the schoolboy Albert Einstein:

One had to cram all this stuff into one's mind whether one liked it or not. This coercion had such a deterring effect that, after I had passed the final examination, I found the consideration of any scientific problem distasteful to me for an entire year.... It is, in fact, nothing short of a miracle that the modern methods of instruction have not yet entirely strangled the holy curiosity of enquiry: for this delicate little plant, aside from stimulation stands mainly in need of freedom: without this it goes to rack and ruin without fail.

Particularly ironic, perhaps, were Einstein's complaints about 'modern methods'. At almost any time we find the blame put upon new-fangled ideas. The abuses repeat themselves. But try as I may, I can find no evidence of a golden age in popular education. Every objection of today can be paralleled from the past, right down to violence and disrespect. Even Shakespeare parodied the older generation's carping – 'I would there were no age between ten and three-and-twenty, or that youth would sleep out the rest; for there is nothing in the between but getting wenches with child, wronging the ancientry, stealing, fighting.'[10] We have precedents from the last century of schoolboy strikes and protest marches. (In 1889 schoolchildren marched through London to demand an end to caning.) At least in our own time there has been no need to use troops to quell school riots as was done at both Eton and Harrow some 150 years ago.

If there never was a heyday in schooling, does this really mean that standards have not declined? So many well-informed and influential people are saying that they have, that our school-leavers are inadequately prepared, that, at least in basic necessities, our young are not as well-trained as they were. The onslaught against modern methods made in the Black Papers struck a chord that was taken up popularly.[11] So many voices joined the authors in agreement. Could they all be wrong? There must have been a reason for the chorus of dissatisfaction in the 1970s. Have there not been Great Debates and government enquiries to prove that there is fire behind the smoke?

Well yes and no. Just over a century ago there was a realisation at government levels of the urgent need for a literate and skilled work force if Britain was to maintain the lead it had gained as an advanced, expanding industrial power. Standards had not fallen, but new needs had arisen and popular education was introduced on the strength of it. In 1870, W. E. Forster proposed enactment in these terms: 'What is our purpose in this Bill? Briefly this, to bring elementary education within the reach of every English home. Upon this speedy provision of elementary education depends our industrial prosperity.' In our own time it has equally been realised that continued prosperity in our post-industrial, technological, pluralist society is going to require some comparable leap forward educationally and that the existing system is inadequate. Regrettably, we have shown less courage, enterprise and optimism than our forebears who backed Mr Forster in 1870. Instead of looking forward in his manner, we have looked back, searching for some former pattern to which we can revert. Instead of identifying the new demands and looking to ways in which the educational system might help to meet them, the Black Paper authors, and others who have boarded their bandwagon, have sought their answer in a mythical past.

It is ironic that whereas the Victorian reformers were radical, progressive and expressed a national self-confidence, the Black Paperists should appear as this manifestation of doubt and regression. Their false alarms about falling standards have recently been systematically dismantled by critics like Nigel Wright in his *Progress in Education*.[12] What I hope to do in this book is to encourage a bolder, fundamental departure in our handling of post-primary education, something that will go beyond mere tinkering with the old machinery in the hope that a few new spare parts will put it right, something, however, that demands an optimism which is not now widely felt, but which our children undeniably deserve.

First, though, let us look a bit more closely at the present crisis of confidence in our education system. Why is it, anxieties over the national economy apart, that the schools have been accused of falling short on their job? The cry of falling standards has probably always been there, but why at this time should it be so intense, and where is the dissatisfaction focused? I shall try to identify a short list of areas of concern, along with some comment on them that may point to the later recommendations of this book.

Notes

1. Criteria for 'an educated man' offered by Robert Conquest, *Fight for Education. A Black Paper*, ed. C. B. Cox and A. E. Dyson, Critical Quarterly Society, 1969, p. 17.

2. Ronald Blythe, *Akenfield*, Allen Lane, 1969.
3. Gerard Holmes, *The Idiot Teacher*, Faber, 1952. (Reissued Spokesman, 1977.)
4. The Newsom Report, *Half Our Future: A Report of the Central Advisory Council for Education (England)*, HMSO, 1963.
5. The Newbolt Report, *The Teaching of English in England*, HMSO, 1921.
6. The Spens Report, *Secondary Education with Special Reference to Grammar and Technical High Schools: Report of the Consultative Committee*, HMSO, 1938.
7. The Norwood Report, *Curriculum and Examinations in Secondary Schools: Report of the Committee of the Secondary School Examination Council*, HMSO, 1943.
8. B. K. Ashby, *Joseph Ashby of Tysoe 1859–1919, A Study of English Village Life*, Cambridge University Press 1961; Merlin Press, 1974.
9. James Kay-Shuttleworth, *Four Periods of Public Education*, Longman, 1862.
10. Shakespeare, *The Winters Tale*, Act IV.
11. C. B. Cox and, A. E. Dyson (eds), *Fight for Education*, Critical Quarterly Society, 1969; *Black Paper Two: The Crisis in Education*, Critical Quarterly Society, 1969; *Black Paper Three: Goodbye Mr Short*, Critical Quarterly Society, 1970; C. B. Cox and Rhodes Boyson (eds), *Black Paper 1975*, J. M. Dent, 1975.
12. Nigel Wright, *Progress in Education*. Croom Helm, 1977.

The crisis of confidence

Attainment levels

Perhaps the most frequently heard complaint from employers
is that they cannot find school-leavers who are proficient in
basic skills, particularly in adding and subtracting, in spelling,
punctuation and sentence construction. Employers with
longer experience and memories claim that they knew the
time when they could expect young people to have mastered
these skills. What they are likely to have overlooked is that in
those days they could expect to choose from some of the best
performers at school. Even twenty-five years ago, fifteen-year-
olds were leaving school and entering employment, leaving
behind a small minority of their fellows to continue at school
and possibly in higher education. Those taken into employment that required literacy and a capacity for basic arith-
metical computation were drawn from the best of those
school-leavers. Successive raisings of the school-leaving age,
increased voluntary staying-on, and the huge expansion of
university and polytechnic places have withheld that sector
from the employment market. The pre-war office junior,
casting pages of accounts, or typing routine letters, has a
counterpart now studying full-time for a higher qualification,
probably a degree. The employer just has to cast his net in
other waters.

What does the net fish up? Those who are older for a start,
since they now must continue in school until after reaching
the age of sixteen. More particularly, employers are interviewing youngsters whose counterparts a generation or two
ago they would never have considered. Where did they go
to? At that time they would have joined the ranks of the vast
armies of unskilled labour. What was required of them was
neither literacy nor numeracy but 'the sweat of their brow'.

8

They were the former navvies, domestic servants, farm workers, the traditional hewers of wood and drawers of water. In a remarkably short time we have seen the simultaneous introduction of mechanisation in every field of work and the reduction in the need for unskilled labour. It seems to have gone unnoticed that nobody now hews wood or draws water. They have become qualified chain-saw mechanics or trained officials of the Water Board. Girls, too, who might formerly have been needed at home to help with large families and who would themselves have settled into early marriage, have competed on the job market.

It is of course very confusing for an employer. He advertises for a bright sixteen-year-old. He interviews a series of healthy young men as tall as himself, or attractive young women, all with fine complexions, well dressed in tasteful fashion, and is then horrified to discover that they don't know where the Amazon is, let alone how long it is, or how to spell its name. What is the world coming to? Yet if he looked out of his window he would not see, as his father might have, either the spotty, undersized errand-boy whistling on his delivery round, or the girl with prematurely thick ankles lugging a laundry basket on her hip, neither of them caring much about the Amazon and nobody expecting them to either. Look at any volume of *Punch* older than the Second World War and the accepted ignorance ('higorance') of the working class, particularly servants, so amusing to 'the educated classes', is abundantly evident.

Within a generation the expectation has totally altered. 'The great unwashed' has disappeared, or been replaced by those who have deliberately rebelled, grown unkempt, ragged or dirty by choice as a protest against something or other, often just against dull respectability. But they are not likely to be the offspring of those known to their masters as 'hoi polloi'. The children of yesterday's labourers are remarkably smart and respectable. And, of course, things are expected of them for which they have no background of recent tradition. New skills are needed and in almost every walk of employment literacy is required. In my own line of business I have seen, for instance, how a school caretaker, who used to be someone

9

who liked children and was handy with mop, shovel and padlock, has been replaced by the 'site supervisor' who needs to operate sophisticated heater installations and fill in complicated returns. I have known an honest, helpful, amiable middle-aged man fail in the job and resign because he was sub-literate and could not manage a task which he would once have been admirably suited for. The standards demanded have risen on every hand.

In the recent Adult Literacy Programme launched by the government to give a new opportunity to those who left school illiterate or sub-literate, over 2 million people have been borne in mind. That is more people than on average fill the football stadiums for league matches every Saturday. Where have they all come from, and why the sudden concern for them? They have all come from the school system, if not in a golden age then certainly from a time before the introduction of the new methods currently under attack. They were always there, but formerly were very well able to conceal their deficiency. The established methods of teaching produced them and until now got away with it. The demands of the technological age have not rendered literacy and numeracy less necessary but quite the reverse. The schools now need a more effective approach if that demand is to be met.

The usefulness of examinations

One paradox in our contemporary crisis of education is that at a time when a cry is going up for higher standards and increased qualifications, there has never before been such a plethora of examining and certificating. Not surprisingly there has been a growing scepticism among those whose responsibility it is to check credentials over the validity of certificates issued by the various boards and universities.

Part of the problem is that when fewer people were certificated, examination records could be used as a means of selection, which is what public examinations originally existed for. Now, however, the majority, if not quite everybody, wants a certificate. Or more accurately, every parent wants their child to have one. There exists a pathetic faith in the efficacy of 'that bit of paper', especially among those who never had one themselves. Douglas, Ross and Simpson, who give detailed research findings on parental expectations in Chapter 12 of *All Our Future*, concluded that 'parents of widely different ages have similar educational aspirations for their children and it seems that they adopt current attitudes towards education rather than carry forward those of their own generation'.[1] Certainly one of their aspirations adopted with current attitudes is that they will leave school with a certificate. Indeed the rapid growth of public examination over the last fifteen years has been largely the result of parental demand. I shall raise the issue of developments in the examination system in a later chapter. The point here is that when I was a boy of sixteen only a minority of my peers took any public examinations, whereas now the great majority take them. The result has been to debase their currency.

As the number of school students entered for examination has risen, so the number of successful candidates has soared. But not only is the public faced with so many certificate holders, they hold certificates in so many different things. Before 1945 it was possible to ask whether a school-leaver held a Matriculation Certificate and if he did, you knew it represented a creditable standard of achievement in a group of basic subjects, including English, maths and a modern language. Nowadays even someone holding five passes at Ordinary Level GCE may turn out to have them in woodwork, photography, history of music, cookery and community studies. In other words, the principal examination has ceased to be descriptive of a general education in what was thought to be the essentials, and has become, in spite of the names *General* Certificate in Education and Certificate of *Secondary* Education, a diversified record of widely varied grades of attainment in widely varied fields of study.

The dissatisfaction with levels of attainment among school-leavers has led some to call for standardised tests to be administered by the Department of Education at certain ages. There is a superficial appearance of logic in this demand: it appears to require objectively stated standards – what might be expected of any child, who is not defective, at a given age; it poses a threat to teachers who do not bring their charges up to the mark, since by their fruits shall they be known; it provides clear short-term goals that will motivate children to improve their performance, in a way that, so it might be claimed, the former 'eleven-plus' examinations did before comprehensive reorganisation abolished them.

A closer look at the probable consequences of such an imposition reveals the dangers of such a reactionary move. It would suggest that children should develop educationally at uniform rates and along identical predestined grooves; it would lead to gradings that, like streaming, would encourage the top at the expense of lowering the lid on the performance of all the others below; it would drive teachers into a concentration of effort upon what can and would be tested to the neglect of less tangible but highly important aspects of learning; it would pander to those who for political reasons would seek to label schools 'good' or 'bad', regardless of the backgrounds outside school that determine so much of what can be attained inside them.

Fortunately, the Secretaries of State in their Green Paper of 1977, categorically stated that they 'reject the idea that rigid and uniform national tests should be applied to all children at certain ages'.[2]

At the other level most carefully looked at by employers, the degree has similarly lost its general standing as the hallmark of a well-trained mind and one needs to ask what it is in. A degree in classics does not speak of the same capabilities on the owner's part as a degree in estate management. Gone are the days when the Civil Service might link a facility in composition of Greek verse with administrative competence. Nowadays it is the *particular* details of the degree that must be taken into account, and even then, many enquirers may be left baffled if they are really wanting that general answer. The questions 'Is she a first-class mind?' and 'Is he a well-rounded individual?' can no longer be answered like that. It may all seem frustratingly fragmented and confusing to someone wanting a simple lead as in grandfather's day.

Readiness for employment

Before the recent proliferation of examinations, an employer could put up in his window the standard notice 'Smart Lad Wanted'. Nowadays he would feel obliged to add 'Must have five O-Levels'. It is not that he would require to use the skills and the knowledge that any particular O-Levels would testify to, but that holding five O-Levels would be the new way of distinguishing the smart lad. The problem for the employer is to know whether the school-leaver is suited to his employment. A local estate agent recently asked for an assistant, stipulating that he must have A-Level Maths. When asked why, he explained that it was to make sure that he could work out the interest rates on mortgages.

Obviously this was an unrealistic demand, the sort that worries parents and in turn their children, who begin to believe that they will be unemployable without A-Level qualifications. It is hard now to convince anxious parents that the majority of school-leavers do not hold any O-Levels, that the average combined O-Level and Grade 1 CSE pass rate expressed nationally for school-leavers is a fraction over one subject per head. So that at the same time as the value of certificates is being debased, indiscriminate employers are asking for more of them.

This seems to be an international trend. Nils Christie, Professor of Criminology at Oslo University,[3] has condemned the same phenomenon and advocated a law to make it an offence to advertise for a qualification that the employer could not demonstrate was related to the demands of the job. This may be a desperate remedy, but one can't resist a sneaking sympathy for the employer who simply asked the school two questions – 'Can he spell? Will he do as he's told?'

In planning the curriculum of a school, the Head will want to take account of the expectations of local and national employment to some degree or other. He may over-react in the face of frantic reports in the Press about complaints from employers who fail to find suitably competent applicants. There is no doubt that any such criticisms are sensationalised.

More sober studies show that these dissatisfactions are less global and strident than the public is led to think.[4] Public outcry, touched off by the Black Papers, led Mrs Thatcher, when Secretary of State for Education, to commission Sir Alan Bullock to enquire into standards of literacy. Instead of the appalling revelations confidently expected by the harbingers of doom, the report, *A Language for Life*, could find no evidence of a decline in standards of English.[5] What it did was to detail at length the higher standards that are needed and ways of reaching them. (This did not prevent one member of the commission, Mr Stuart Froome, from denying the evidence, like an inverted Galileo, and sticking to his original conviction of falling standards.[6]) The Bullock Report certainly did not advocate, as a leader in the *Leicester Mercury* claimed in a headline that it did, 'Stick to the three R's.'[7] Its demands were more diverse and more exacting. There is little doubt that the enquiry into the teaching of mathematics recently authorised by Mrs Williams will reach similar conclusions: that the standards now needed by society have risen steeply and that the best of modern methods will need to be extended if we are to meet them.

But in the meantime what do employers look for? Faultless spelling and unquestioning obedience? Hardly. In a later chapter I shall consider the prognosis of demands upon our schools in the immediate future. At present, apart from specific requirements in specific jobs, general expectations are still remarkably straightforward. In a study carried out for the Leicestershire Education Committee,[8] Mrs E. T. Keil of Loughborough University reported that employers expect their recruits to make their mark if they exhibit three particular characteristics. They need to be hardworking, skilled and adaptable.

These seem to be three eminently reasonable expectations on the part of employers. The problem is that no examinations at present test these qualities and so no certificates with national currency can testify to them. A top-grade pass is no guarantee that the student is going to work hard at anything other than the subject in question: he may love studying Tudor history but hate making abstracts of company reports, or love maths but hate computer print-outs. Some students sail through examinations without working hard at all.

So the employer looking for these characteristics will have to rely on his own assessment of candidates and reports from the schools. There is much room for doubt over the competence of many employers to apply suitable diagnostic tests to their applicants. Too many still seem to use tests of attainment for which the candidates may not have been prepared, tests that are too often at variance with the qualities and competences being looked for. It is no comfort to acknowledge that they have learnt to compile these inappropriate tests from their recollections of how schools operated. What must be faced is a decline of confidence among employers in what they can find out from the school system today.

Relevance of the curriculum

What *do* they teach them at school these days? Not an uncommon question, suggesting that whatever is going on in school, it has left increasingly large gaps in what a school-leaver should be expected to know. The trouble is that as the sum total and diversity of human knowledge has expanded, quite explosively in our own day, it is increasingly difficult to find agreement about what should be selected from it as the essential core for school students to learn.

I shall draw out the implications of this situation in Chapter 4, as they seem to me to be considerable.

I shall also explore later the differences of emphasis between a curriculum of what is taught and a curriculum of what is learnt. It is sufficient here to say that if 'curriculum' is taken to mean the aggregate of what is taught within a school, then somebody has to draw up its contents, unless (and this can all too easily happen) it merely grows out of what was there before with neither aim nor control other than the syllabus requirements of the public examinations. Even then, the range and variety of subject syllabuses has also grown to the point where if nothing else determines the curriculum, a Head and the staff have to choose between the different

ning boards available to them, and then between the
cts that may be offered for examination, and then
ween the alternative syllabuses there may be in any subject.
Severe doubts about the readiness of school-leavers to face
tne world has led to heated argument about who should
control the curriculum. It has been maintained that this is too
important a public concern to be left entirely to teachers.
Parents, governors, politicians, employers, even students,
have all made their claim to a share in curriculum control. Of
course there is a sense in which, whatever is said or decreed
by anyone else, the curriculum, what happens in the classrooms, is finally determined by the teacher and the class. In
that sense, the teacher and student do have ultimate control.
But everyone except the most eccentric or obtuse, is open to
influence and the teachers, if not the students, will respond to
reasonable pressure. Pressures have therefore been exerted.

Unfortunately, the pressures have not produced any resultant direction. Some pressures cancel each other out and many
are so intermittent as to cause lurching. In 1976 the Prime
Minister, Mr Callaghan, none less, launched what he hoped
would be the Great Debate on the curriculum. There were
televised discussions, regional conferences and innumerable
minor confrontations. All interested parties and all major
political parties were involved. Mrs Shirley Williams, the
Secretary of State for Education, travelled tirelessly round
the country, showing a commendable capacity for listening.
But what she must have heard, certainly what was heard in the
public debate, was mostly a series of prepared statements.
No consensus emerged other than a platitudinous Green
Paper.[9] What was needed was a lead into drastic, radical
revision of post-primary education. What we got was a
thoroughly unimaginative set of reassurances, designed presumably to keep everyone happy. A very timid mouse it was
after a mountainous labour.

One merciful outcome of this *soi-disant* Great Debate,
was a demonstration by default that there was no likelihood
of our being saddled with a centrally controlled curriculum.
There had been calls for one, or at least a centrally defined
core-curriculum, a central block of compulsory learning,

around which could be added the studies selected by some more domestic means at the school. There has been a healthy wariness in this country of any possible machinery by which a government could control what was taught in schools, or by what methods. There are too many shades of totalitarian governments abroad bolstered by a close control over what was set before the young. Even in modern France the Napoleonic grip still persists in schools.

Behaviour and discipline

In recent years, considerable publicity has been given to incidents of violence in schools, violence between students, violence directed towards teachers and by teachers towards students. It has always gone on to some degree, though formerly less fuss was made about it. However, in the past, it was only at selective schools, grammar and independent, that the pupils grew to be larger than their teachers and there any sustained insubordination could always be dealt with by expulsion. It was only in rare cases that within the elementary school a boy would grow strong enough to put his teacher on top of a cupboard and leave her there, as did the rebel described by Laurie Lee in *Cider With Rosie*.[10]

But with successive raisings of the school-leaving age and improved standards of health, Jack has grown as big as his master, and Jill as her mistress. Outbreaks of violence and vandalism, when they occur in school, have become more difficult to curb or contain. Attention has been drawn to the increase of physical violence between girls.

If there has been an increase of violence and vandalism, few would claim that it is confined to the schools. Many more, however, would attribute their origin to schools. Even hooliganism on the football stands has been blamed on lax discipline in schools, the teachers accused of trendy permissiveness. The whole hue and cry about the breakdown of law and order has inevitably led to demands for more rigorous control and painful punishment in schools.

It could be argued that the violence and destruction is not

much new as misdirected. I and my generation were trained pretty thoroughly between the ages of fourteen and nineteen in violence and destruction. That it was directed towards Germany and Japan made it respectable, of course. We were not too sure at that age of our reasons for going to war, but it channelled our aggressiveness much more effectively even than football.

Be that as it may, and whether or not the rate of increase in illegal violence and vandalism is exaggerated by the increase of publicity, police arrests and convictions, the problem remains of how to deal with it. In looking to any part that schools can play in this, I find that much light is thrown on the subject by Mia Kellmer Pringle, Director of the National Children's Bureau.[11] In a brilliant and lucid paper 'The roots of violence and vandalism' (which should be recommended reading for every teacher, parent, governor and county councillor), she argues that there are four basic emotional needs common to all of us and continuous throughout life. They are the need for: (i) love and security; (ii) new experiences; (iii) praise and recognition; (iv) responsibility. She then makes this telling observation:

> If one of these basic needs remains unmet – or inadequately met – then one of two reactions follows: fight or flight, attack or withdrawal. Society reacts much more strongly to those children and young adults who respond by fighting, attacking – probably because this is seen as a challenge to authority; because it arouses feelings of aggression and revenge; and because by force we can control its outward expression, at least temporarily. But there is little evidence that meeting aggression with coercion brings about any lasting change, rather, a vicious circle is set up – with escalating violence and inevitably more forceful control.

In the past, this final escalation and more forceful control could end with the teacher winning, in the sense of regaining command. After all, a group of twelve-year-olds, unversed in how to offer united resistance, had little chance against grown men and women, armed and experienced in the techniques of physical and verbal retaliation. Subjugation could be ensured, if not by the individual teacher, then by the school hierarchy.

But those days are over. If teachers succumb to the pressures for 'more forceful control' the escalation will lead to the horrific situation now common in the big cities of the USA where armed police patrol the school corridors and examine passes. The alternative is to work for a radically different *modus vivendi* in school, a total change in relationships. And the schools will not solve the problems of violence and vandalism in society any more than they have caused them. Even the amelioration of the situation that we might contribute to cannot be achieved on our own.

Student protest

In case it should be thought that the crisis of confidence in the school system is confined to the generation of parents, employers and the Press, I want to conclude with a reflection upon the response of the user, the school student. The violence and vandalism just referred to is unlikely to emerge on any scale in the school where the students are satisfied that their needs are being met. Most of the public criticism of schools is in terms of the needs of any party other than the school students. This, of course, is one very potent source of any discontent expressed by the student. Everybody's interests are considered except his own.

I have already implied that society has failed to adjust its image of the school student since the last two post-war raisings of the school-leaving age. I use the term 'school student', for this reason, that we need to mark the norm of secondary school seniors as sixteen, not fourteen as it was when I was that age. Fourteen is the average age of the present-day secondary student, not twelve, as it was when the image still current was moulded. A twelve-year-old can be thought of as a 'school-kid', with cap and satchel: a sixteen-year-old is legally entitled to own a motorised vehicle, be married, have children, earn regular money. Moreover, most school students of fifteen and sixteen are the first in their family history not to have been out at work since fourteen in field, factory, shop or pit, accorded some degree of adult status, collecting a wage, however small, that confirmed his or her necessary contribution to the national and domestic economy. Nowadays the whole system tells them unmistakably that they are not needed. Even when they do leave school, increasing numbers of them are finding that there is no work for them.

It is a wonder that more of them do not show open resentment of being treated like this. We cannot overlook the long tradition of working-class feeling that school is an intrusion into family life, 'irrelevant to the central business of living'.[12]

I was speaking to a bus conductor who had complained about rudeness from some school students. 'When I was at school,' he said, 'we were stood in line and did as we were told.' I asked him when he had left school. 'Fourteen,' he said. I then pointed out that this was the age at which, in a Leicestershire upper-school, I received them. 'Did you stand in line and do as you were told at sixteen?' I asked. 'Not likely,' I was told. To him they had just been school-kids, and some adults are extraordinarily rude to them, still expecting automatic respect in return. They are lucky to get no more than a shrug of indifference.

But we have been no better within the teaching profession. Each raising of the school-leaving age has been announced years in advance. Each occasion has been heralded as a grand opportunity for a completely fresh approach to schooling in the last year. Each date-line has been passed with no real change of approach and teachers protesting that they were being forced to put up with the ineducable who neither wanted to be there nor were themselves wanted. At the best, curricula were revamped, but almost universally the new strata of school students were getting the same old things as before. However loud the complaints have been outside school that new trends were threatening the established order, the evidence is that hardly anything has changed at root. With considerable uniformity, what the young find in school is what they always used to find.

What did the new stayers find, that was all too like what they were already familiar with? For far too many of them, what they found was that they were obliged to follow a timetable of subjects they had not chosen to study, in groups they had not chosen to join, with teachers they had expressed no desire to study with, being told the answers to questions they had not asked, forced by bells to go to rooms they were directed to at times that bore no relationship to what they might be learning. They were frequently chivvied, if not bawled at or lectured to, and were probably expected to wear a 'uniform' as well. When I was supervising graduate students on teaching practice, I used to urge them to spend a day attached to one particular class and to follow it closely from lesson to lesson. It gave a totally different perspective to any they gained in their teacher role, and more to the point, the experience of fragmentation left them exhausted.

As teachers, we are not very good at knowing what is really happening to our students.[13] It is not then surprising that those outside the school may also be unaware. To them, student unrest, whether manifesting itself in violence, or in orderly protest, may appear to be a failure on the part of teachers and parents to keep them under control. A closer inspection might reveal a deep and long-felt exasperation among these school students at the folly of the elders. What is more remarkable is that the young are so tolerant and long-suffering on the whole.

Notes

1. J. W. B. Douglas, J. M. Ross and H. R. Simpson, *All Our Future: A Longitudinal Study of Secondary Education*, Peter Davies, 1968.
2. *Education in Schools. A Consultative Document*, HMSO, 1977.
3. Nils Christie, *If the School Wasn't There*, Oslo University Press.
4. For instance, Fogelman in *Britain's Sixteen-Year-Olds*, ed. K. Fogelman, National Children's Bureau, 1976. The National Child Development Study, one of the most extensive pieces of long-term research, enquired of 11,650 parents in 1974 whether they were satisfied with their children's schooling when they reached the age of sixteen: 66 per cent expressed satisfaction, 26 per cent were satisfied in some respects but not in others, and only 8 per cent were dissatisfied.

5. The Bullock Report, *A Language for Life: Report of the Committee of Enquiry Appointed by the Secretary of State for Education and Science*, HMSO, 1975.

6. Ibid.

7. The *Leicester Mercury*, 14 February 1975.

8. E. T. Keil, *Becoming a Worker*. Obtainable from the Director of Education. Leicestershire County Council. Glenfield. Leicester.

9. *Education in Schools, A Consultative Document*. HMSO, 1977.

10. Laurie Lee, *Cider with Rosie*, The Hogarth Press, 1959.

11. Mia Kellmer Pringle, *The Roots of Violence and Vandalism*, National Children's Bureau, 1973. (Reprinted from *Concern*, the journal of the Bureau.)

12. B. Jackson and D. Marsden, *Education and the Working Class*, Routledge and Kegan Paul, 1962.

13. Ibid. Ch. 6 offers some disconcerting evidence.

3 1945-1975
Changes and tinkerings

The British are inclined towards piecemeal reform rather than revolutionary change. This is, in general, more conducive to a comfortable life, but it does run the severe risk of meandering, of changing first one thing and then another without any clear, co-ordinating, long-term aim. Piecemeal reform is desirable where there exist coherent, accepted principles for guidance which can then be applied to the circumstances of the time. But since the prophetic Education Act of 1944, our education system has lurched heavily in various directions, responding to various pressures, with no observable consistency of purpose. This may be the price of parliamentary democracy. It certainly leaves wide open the question of where we go from here.

I want to string together brief accounts of ten of these developments in order to ask whether they reveal any consistent approach and whether cumulatively they point towards a necessary and concerted leap forward that may justify our continuing to oblige parents over the rest of this century to send their children to school rather than find them other occupation.

1. Comprehensivisation

An ugly word, but one with a clear meaning – the reorganisation of schools of various kinds so as to provide in each one of them the curricula appropriate for *all* the children of any age group. The story of this movement has been chronicled with care and can be read elsewhere.[1] The point I wish to make here is that the forces behind the movement have been various, educational and political. The changes have been largely organisational, leaving enormous potential for new developments arising from the comprehensive schools. This potential is hardly tapped as yet.

The arguments for comprehensive reorganisation are as old as those for secondary education as such, first breathing official air in the Hadow Report of 1926.[2] Campaigning started then, notably with action by London Labour teachers. They persuaded Herbert Morrison to carry the LCC with him in 1935, to support the idea in principle of a common secondary school, the 'multilateral school' as it was then called. However, the order of the day was still common elementary schooling, topped for the selected few by grammar schooling, with its highly competitive entry at eleven. The 'eleven-plus' selection examination was to predominate for years to come, is still operated in local authorities which maintain grammar schools, and still advocated by those who feel its disappearance has led to lower standards in primary schools.

The political motivation for comprehensive reorganisation sprang from a conviction that division of eleven-year-olds into a hierarchy of different kinds of schools was decided more by the social background of the children than by their educational potential. It was hard for working-class children to get into grammar school and even harder to stay the course until eighteen, let alone proceed to university.[3] Furthermore, the successful grammar school pupil, whatever his or her origin, was destined for the middle classes, thus confirming the function of the grammar school for the working class as an escape ladder. This was felt to be socially divisive.

The educational motivation for reform was related, in that it denied the existence of innate differences in children's mental capacity that could so neatly correspond to the categories of the school system. The division into separate schools not only put a seal on the class differences of children, but it effectively determined the general level of their educational development. This meant that the vast majority of children were doomed to under-achieve.

Taken together, these arguments pointed to gross social injustice. The demand was for 'parity in education' and for 'equal opportunity'. Predictably, opponents of the reform distorted this by representing it as a claim for equality of ability, or a demand that all children should be treated alike.[4] It was genuinely hard for many, perhaps still influenced by Samuel Smiles and by images of Industrious Apprentices taking the opportunities neglected by the Idle Apprentices, to understand that the way could not be wide open for any boy or girl to get on if they were determined to.

It took the social upheaval of the war and the resultant desire to build a better world to inspire R. A. Butler's 1944 Education Act and open up the way for comprehensive schooling. Unfortunately, when the first wave of purpose-built comprehensive schools opened in the late 1950s, much of the drive to bring grammar schools, technical schools and secondary modern schools under one roof, ended just there. In other words, intricate planning and vast sums of money were invested in the buildings, equipment and organisation of intake, but nothing corresponding to this was applied to preparing new and appropriate arrangements inside the new schools once the children got there.

Inside the large new comprehensive, the child was streamed into one course or another, virtually remaining a grammar school pupil or a secondary modern pupil. It was rather more sophisticated than that, and viewed *in total*, the curriculum was impressive since nearly everything was there, somewhere – Greek, Bricklaying, Physics, Shorthand. But the choices were for the most part very limited, determined largely by the student's point of entry.[5] It was a step forward: an increased number who had 'failed' the eleven-plus were enabled to have an opportunity to follow a grammar school curriculum. Late-developers took clutches of O-Levels and joined the sixth form.

What it demonstrated most clearly at that time was how many more will avail themselves of new opportunities once offered than the forecasters plan for. The comprehensive school made a fifth year available long before the school-leaving age was raised to fifteen. Because it was there to be seen, because it did not involve transfer to another school or college of further education, many more opted to remain for an additional year than would have done so in the former secondary modern school. At Crown Woods School in 1960, two years after opening, it was found that there were twice as many fifth-formers as had been predicted, and projecting this number into the new sixth form meant enlarging the school to well beyond its intended maximum of 2,000.

The comprehensives did that, but they failed to provide any new approach to teaching. What went on in the classrooms was very much what had gone on before under the different roofs. There was enormous pressure to demonstrate to the world that all that could be accomplished in the grammar schools could be encompassed in the new comprehensive. This competition forced the comprehensives in many ways to ape the grammar school image. Strict attention was paid to academic performance, homework, uniform, house contests, rituals and formalities. Jokes were made by the onlookers about announcements such as – 'From today there will be a new tradition'. But there was little likelihood in that atmosphere of any departure from previous styles of teaching and learning. In any case, the teachers were no new breed: they were recruited or redirected from the old schools, all too often bringing with them their mutual hostilities and cherishing them.

In passing, I would note that inadequate valedictions were paid to the secondary modern schools. Undeniably, by their very nature, they limited the opportunities open to their intake of children. But at their best, before the burden of public examinations settled on their backs, they fostered caring personalised relationships both between their staff and students and within their neighbourhood. They could be small enough to belong in a community. (They could also at their worst be large, brutal and drab.)

Finally, the whole point of a comprehensive school is that it should cater for the full range of talent in its neighbourhood, in the belief that its members will rise to improved opportunities and benefit from the mingling instead of the segregation of classes and abilities. There is an almost Orwellian flavour of humbug in the notion of comprehensive and grammar schools co-existing in one area and drawing their intakes from it. This inevitably means that the grammar school is a grammar school (to which some parents may 'choose' to send their children), while the other school will become a secondary modern school. If it masquerades as a comprehensive it will be large, with all the problems of a secondary modern school writ large. Yet large numbers of the electorate have been deceived by politicians who have peddled this idea in the name of parental choice. The great majority of parents under such an organisation would have no effective choice, no option but to consign their children to the 'creamed' comprehensive.

Successive governments shied away from merging grammar schools into comprehensives until the Labour government of 1965 ordered all authorities to submit plans for comprehensive reorganisation. Some delayed indefinitely. The Tory government of 1970 withdrew the order. Most local authorities have gone ahead anyway, too often with merger plans that have turned out to be dogs' dinners, coercing too many teachers where wooing them was called for.

In that wooing might have lain the chance of a transformation of attitudes towards learning, towards the upper secondary student, towards fellow teachers in a staff team. As it is, a golden opportunity was lost, management and organisation have been the watchwords of the day, and the battle for humanising school has yet to be won.

2. Unstreaming: mixed-ability groups

One reason for the term 'comprehensive' being accepted in the 1930s in place of 'multilateral' was that it suggested opportunities of a completely new mix in school. As we have seen, the comprehensives, far from taking that opportunity for a fresh ferment, turned out to be multilateral, many-sided, after all. Consequently, those who saw what was happening in the 1950s and the 1960s began almost at once to campaign against streaming in schools. Streaming is the division of children, according to performance or estimates of ability, into classes of like attainment. These classes then take on a rank order. No school, however ingenious in its labelling, can conceal from its children what this pecking order is. This was one of the atrocities of the first big comprehensive schools.

There could be up to eighteen streams. In the 1950s David Holbrook touched the public and professional consciences for the first time over the dehumanising effect of dumping kids 'down the C stream' in secondary moderns.[6] But what is the feeling of being in the C stream of a three-stream school compared to realising at the age of eleven that you have been weighed in the balance and placed in the fifteenth stream of a sixteen-stream school? That must feel like living with your family down the bottom of an eighteenth-century coal-mine.

The way in which streaming was a reflection of the selective system and the way in which the large comprehensive schools were accentuating the division was most forcibly publicised by Brian Jackson with a book entitled *Streaming: An Education System in Miniature.*[7] The most consistent, practical and thoughtful campaigning for unstreaming has been conducted by the editorial board of the journal *Forum*.[8] Unstreaming, obviously, entails grouping students in parallel classes, each with a wide spread of ability. A half-way compromise is to set up clusters of such parallel classes within a limited band of ability, thereby reducing the number of rungs on the ladder for the students (you only know you are Band 4, rather than say N stream) and reducing the spread of abilities in any one class for the teacher. A fully unstreamed class would confront the teacher in one room with both his potential university candidate and the potential non-examined (non-examinable) early leaver.

It would seem axiomatic that a teacher faced for the first time with an unstreamed class would need to use a totally new technique if, as is likely, he has been accustomed to teaching to the pace and understanding of the average in his class. There is a danger in any class, however finely streamed, that at one extreme certain members will be bored (and subversive) because they can outstrip the majority, and at the other extreme their counterparts who are troublesome (and uninterested) because they can't keep up. The wider the spread of ability, the more marked the problem.

Therefore, teachers need to be persuaded to plan and retrain for this innovation. They need encouragement and help. All too often the change has been thrust upon them without their receiving either, with consequences I shall take up at the end of this chapter.

To handle mixed-ability classes effectively, the teacher needs a variety of material and a knowledge of a whole range of activities that can be promoted as appropriate for his different students. Where is he going to find these materials or make them? Who is going to arrange for him to discuss their uses, try them out, exchange these ideas with colleagues? And when will the time be found? Is this where external agencies come into play?

3. The Schools Council

The problem of how to bring about changes in what went on in the classroom once reorganisation of the schools was beginning to come about posed a real problem. We have prided ourselves on the autonomy of the classroom teacher: after all advice and pressure, he has always determined his own style. But if this resulted, as it often did, in a refusal to change his tried and successful methods, even when altered circumstances were crying out for such a change, what could be done? Nobody wished to see some externally devised scheme that would prescribe the content and procedure of his lessons day by day.

In the event, the government's Department of Education and Science created in 1964 a Schools Council to review and reform curriculum and examinations. Its terms of reference are interesting in the light of this chapter's consideration. The Schools Council was...

> ...to uphold and interpret the principle that each school should have the fullest possible measure of responsibility for its own work, with its own curriculum and teaching method based on the needs of its own pupils and evolved by its own staff; and to seek, through co-operative study of common problems, to assist all who have individual or joint responsibilities for, or in connection with, the schools' curricula and examinations to co-ordinate their actions in harmony with this principle.

Control of the Schools Council is in the hands of those working in the educational service: teachers, inspectors, local authorities, unions, universities. Their work has included these main activities: issuing pamphlets and working papers of suggestions for curriculum development; urging local authorities, successfully, to set up Teachers' Centres where staff from the schools in the area can meet and organise new teaching approaches and materials between themselves; setting up research and development projects; publishing materials produced by these projects; advocating production of technological equipment found necessary by teachers for their developments.

Some of the most influential promotions of the Schools Council are outlined in the next three sections of this chapter. There is no denying the influence upon teachers' thinking of several of the projects of the Schools Council. With time, however, it came to be felt that the most effective curriculum development was that promoted within a particular school.

School-based curriculum development was most likely to occur through the enthusiastic lead of the head teacher. In fact, it would never get off the ground without positive support from the Head. The most spectacular innovations have occurred when a Head has arrived direct from service with the Schools Council or some allied project to plan a new school, as did Tim McMullen at Countesthorpe in Leicestershire and Geoffrey Cooksey at Stantonbury in Milton Keynes. It is sad that these appointments have been so few and their achievements so isolated and unusual. After all, as is pointed out by Becher and Maclure in their recent book *The Politics of Curriculum Change*, 'almost any outrage becomes a tradition if it can be nursed through infancy'.[9]

4. Teachers' Centres

On reflection, I realise that when I started teaching, the staff of one school had virtually no contact with colleagues at any other unless they were involved in sports fixtures. The necessary exchange of visits precipitated by the introduction of teacher-controlled examinations in 1965, discussed in the next section, had the effect of a bombshell. Teachers actually looked into each other's staffrooms and discussed each other's schemes of work. It caused more flutter than being invited into a strange neighbour's home and being taken to inspect the bedrooms and the contents of the wardrobes.

The spread of Teachers' Centres from about the same time and into the 1970s promoted a more informal exchange between teachers from different schools within one area. They provided a combined social and working atmosphere: teachers could use them to relax and chat over a cup of tea or at a bar, and to get down to business. Usually they have facilitated both meetings organised by teachers themselves and courses for which tutors have been engaged. The key figure has been the Centre Leader or Warden, appointed by the local education authority, either by secondment from one of its schools or from outside on a permanent appointment. This Warden has had to enquire tactfully at local schools into teachers' curriculum needs, interests or problems and try to meet them by constructing programmes, mounting exhibitions and bringing in speakers and consultants.

Second to the Centre Leader has always come the curriculum workshop (some would see the reverse priority). Here would be a bank of resources for teaching – publications, film strips, equipment for audio-visual uses, and often the most useful hardware in the range of reprographics.

Never before have teachers talked about their work so extensively. How much of the talk has led to any change in classroom practice it is difficult to say. A lot of it has undoubtedly led not to change but to a reinforcement of attitudes, some of them heavily prejudiced.

One person at least whose teaching approach will have been fundamentally affected by the experience of each Teachers' Centre, is its Leader. There is, however, no record of how many of them have returned to regular school teaching. It is to be suspected that many, most regrettably, have seen the move as one of promotion out of the classroom in a direction heading away from it rather than back to where the action is and the real changes, if they are yet to come, are to be made.

31

5. Teacher-controlled examining: the Certificate of Secondary Education (CSE) and Mode III examination

The old secondary modern schools had the freedom to teach whatever they felt was appropriate to their own boys and girls in their own locality. Diverse creative activities were promoted as a result. After a decade of such freedom, 1945–55, it was clear that, cut off from the opportunities of the grammar schools, the most able or ambitious in the secondary moderns could still work for and pass a respectable batch of GCE O-Levels. As the demand for this privilege increased, not only did the number of secondary modern students passing O-Levels increase but so did the number who failed it. That is to say that numbers of them forsook the more interesting activities a school could provide in order to grind away diligently at an examination they could not pass. It was a sad sight, and teachers and parents turned increasingly in the next decade, 1955–65, to other, simpler examinations, whose Boards enjoyed a brief period of popularity.

Many of the syllabuses of these minor examinations were educationally trivial. Concern over this, and the continued pressure from employers and parents for certification of some at least of that majority of school-leavers who never reached GCE O-Level, led the newly formed Schools Council to recommend a new Certificate of Secondary Education. This CSE was to be administered by regional boards, but its contents and conduct were to be controlled by the teachers who used it.

The CSE was intended for that 25 per cent of sixteen-year-olds next to the top 25 per cent who took GCE O-Levels. It was to be awarded in single subjects, each with a division into five grades. Grade One would register a standard expected of candidates who would have passed O-Level had they taken it; Grade Four would correspond to the average standard expected of the whole sixteen-year-old population; Grade Five would be a little below that. Clearly, it was not intended that this examination should be used with much more than half the school population.

I opened my first school in 1965, the year that CSE was launched. Sir John Newsom, whose report *Half Our Future*, had given added publicity to the neglect and consequent under-achievement of half our schoolchildren only the year before, came to our official opening. He was, as always, infectiously enthusiastic, but at one point he took me aside with a look of great anxiety. 'This new exam,' he said. 'They all want to use it. Don't go putting my Newsom children in for it, will you.'[10]

It was a vain plea, in the national sense. Soon the exam dominated school. We are now seeing schools where, since the raising of the school-leaving age to sixteen, virtually all students who are there in the summer of their fifth year sit for public examinations.

One significant feature of the CSE was that it was not to be a Pass or Fail examination, but a grading device that would give a certificate of performance. Unfortunately, many employers, who looked only for a label of Pass or Fail and were less interested in what the certificate was actually describing, dismissed the CSE as a 'failed exam'.

The other most significant element in the CSE was that of its Mode III examinations. The normal mode of examining had always been that of the board issuing a subject syllabus, later setting an examination in it, marking the scripts with its own examiners and issuing results against its own standards. A second mode offered allowed the school to propose its own syllabus. If this was approved, the board would then set and mark an examination on it. Mode III enabled the school to submit its own syllabus (singly or jointly with any other schools who cared to form a consortium); if approved, the school would then submit its own examination papers and mark schemes; when the board approved these, the examination was set, marked initially by the teachers internally and then moderated by an external examiner appointed by the board.

Mode III undoubtedly enabled teachers to motivate their students to longer and fuller study of subjects that might otherwise have flagged. Also, because it made possible the examination of course work carried out over a year or more,

Mode III was seen as a means of giving credit where it was due, not just to performance in the examination hall.

The ill-effect of Mode III was that it permitted a proliferation of idiosyncratic syllabuses, many with titles so obscure as to be meaningless to an employer, thus bringing the CSE as a whole into disrepute. Also, it was not understood that Mode III was externally moderated by the boards, and only undertaken to syllabuses and examination schemes meeting their approval. Mode III came to be seen as a sort of do-it-yourself certificate.

My main point here, though, is that perhaps in spite of the opportunities of Mode III and course-work submissions, the spread of examined work in schools has imprisoned school students largely in the memorisation of information. To far too many teachers, often under attack for imprecise aims and low standards, examination courses meant respectability. A sure-fire defence for a teacher against head teacher, governor, parent or other would-be critic (not least the disenchanted student who says, 'Why are we doing this, Miss?') is to retort – 'Ah, they need this for The Examination.' The 1970s backlash over standards has driven teachers to examinations, very often to the detriment of learning.

6. Resource-based learning

The impetus of the Schools Council and other curriculum projects drew the attention of teachers, if no more, to the alternatives to the stock classroom techniques of chalk-and-talk and working from the book. Other resources for learning were introduced to schools by field officers of the large projects, by local authorities' advisers and by the Teacher Centres. These included films, filmstrips, tapes, microfilm information and various kinds of printed material other than books. Most popular of all were packs, or kits, of several kinds of material for use on a single topic. Publishers saw this as a distinct threat to the traditional use of course books, and they too began to put packs of topic materials on to the market.

The Schools Council and publishers have issued pamphlets and books on the detailed use of such material.[11] Gradually, the emphasis has shifted from the imports of the external 'change-agent', to the potential for self-help within the schools or between groups of schools in one area.

There can be little doubt that where these innovations have had impact, changes have taken place in the ways in which schoolchildren learn. And indeed for those teachers involved, changes have occurred in their ways of learning. Teachers and students have pursued enquiries into new ranges of information, learning to locate and retrieve what they want to find out, learning by increased attempts to make and do rather than just giving and absorbing inert facts. New realms have been opened by the encouragement to embark upon group discussions of selected materials. Many a teacher has been marked for life after grappling with Lawrence Stenhouse's materials and the concept of 'neutral chairmanship'.

All to the good. But quite apart from that submerged sector of the teachers' iceberg upon whom none of this has had any effect, if only because they never heard of it, many have used new resources, not so much to sharpen and satisfy that appetite for new experience, learning by problem-solving and fresh sensation, as to squeeze unrelated scraps of information into their students, for subsequent testing. Worse still, the new range of techniques was often debased into entertainment intended to keep the less scholarly quiet and happy between 9 a.m. and 4 p.m. One clear lesson from the whole movement was that there was no such thing as teacher-proof material. All of it was open to abuse, and no teacher could in the end avoid thinking through the purpose for which he was intending to use his resources. Kids get tired with film shows and the novelty wears off glossy new 'packs' as soon as it is apparent that they are only playing about with them.

7. Raising the school-leaving age

Plenty of notice was given to schools that the school-leaving age would be raised in 1972 from fifteen to sixteen. All political parties were committed to the move. The DES and local authorities organised preparatory courses and conferences for the teachers. But there was vacillation: protests were made that large numbers of boys and girls had reached the ceiling of their educability already by fifteen and were eager to leave school. It was argued that a further year would waste their time, be resented and lead to turbulence that it would be unfair to expect teachers to cope with. The same arguments had been advanced when the leaving age was twelve, and with each successive raising of the age. But now they were nearly full grown and not so easily coerced. There were worries that discipline would break down.

The trouble was that the sector of the school population who would have left at fifteen but would now have to stay on, were marked off and identified to their teachers and to themselves. They were known as the RoSLA pupils. Where trouble was predicted from them they usually obliged by living up to the forecast. There was least trouble in schools which avoided creating a block whose main hope lay in getting out of school.

The situation exposed the extent to which schools still categorised their students, particularly the way in which a set of predominantly academic aims polarised them into two camps, the academic, who bought the package, and the unacademic, who either agreed to grin and bear it, much as they might in the lower echelons of employment, or else rejected it and lived in a state of intermittent skirmish with the authorities. It is these latter, who feel that school is not for them, that we have failed. They are the ones who will not wear uniform, who smoke in the toilets, who swear in front of, and even at, the teachers. They resent having to be where they are told to be when they are told to be there. They don't seem ashamed of having amorous relationships, are not prepared to work without knowing precisely what is in it for them, and display no interest in the good name of the school. They are many a good strict teacher's nightmare.

Yet, they are not all violent or delinquent, even if they contain and tolerate those few who are. They are in fact remarkably like the young people out of school and at work a year or two ago, ordinary people who are prepared to give in return for reasonable recompense and if they are not shoved around too much. They just resent being retained as school-kids, subjected to inexplicable regulations, lectured at, even still subjected to corporal punishment. If we watched them and listened to them a little more patiently we might find them telling us something crucially significant about education, school, employment and living.

The new age of leaving has by now become accepted in the sense that no public voices are calling any longer, as they were in 1973–74, for it to be lowered again. One suspects, however, that this is largely because of the problem of unemployment and the fact that school at least houses large numbers who would otherwise be swelling the dole queues. However, it has not answered the problem for those fifteen- and sixteen-year-olds who find themselves in school doing the same old things that they had done before, or else using their inventive talents to devise new forms of idling.

All that has been raised so far in this chapter is evidence that new opportunities for learning have too often been pushed aside to make way for more instruction and examination.

8. Participation and management

Demand for a greater say in the creation of the conditions in which we live and work have been part of the public awareness of democracy outside school. Not surprisingly, these expecta-tions have found their way into schools. In the case of teachers, much of this has resulted from participation in union affairs. What is more surprising is that in the case of the school students there has been so little specific demand for participa-tion in the decision-making at school. It may be that a lot of undirected pupil protest, condemned as indiscipline, has been a crude form of demand for recognition of a more constructive potential. In spite of a National Union of School Students having existed for some years, it has been slow to assist its members in voicing their demands in positive and acceptable ways.

I shall write more later about the changing role of the Head.[12] There are still those outside who expect the Head to rule with a rod of iron, to be supreme dictator. But to some degree or other, Heads have come to see the value of power sharing, even though by contract they must accept ultimate public responsibility. To a large extent this has been forced upon them by the increased size and complexity of the schools they have to run. The early purpose-built comprehensives met the obvious problem of size with strongly constructed frameworks of departmental heads and house heads. There was then a considerable task of management for which at first Heads had no experience. They had to play it by ear. But it was patently obvious that the number and multiplicity of decisions needed daily in an organisation of that size could not be taken or vetted by any one person. A division of decision levels had to be made.

A variety of solutions evolved. In most of them the Head operated through some form of inner cabinet, with deputies and heads of certain major departments and pastoral units. The process of evolution of a power system could be complicated and painful. It was also difficult to keep track of: only rarely did a school have the services of a trained observer to advise them of what was happening.[13] Certainly there was nobody to *tell* them what to do.

Unfortunately, the problem was too rapidly turned into a virtue. Advice from management consultancy was sought and given to good effect. But the idea of Heads and senior teachers as business executives proved seductive. There followed a proliferation of courses and a spate of new jargon. Some of it has been helpful, and nobody could deny the desirability of training for senior staffs. Heads, in particular, can never learn by 'sitting next to Nelly'. All this has been an advance. But it has not avoided the danger of making a school more like a factory than a place to foster learning and human growth. The analogy with industry soon breaks down and there is a profound danger when management techniques are applied in such a way as to treat school students as either products or shop-floor workers. We have allowed increasing reference to school-leavers as the 'products' of school to go without indignant rebuttal. Schools have been urged to step up production and attend more carefully to marketing their goods. This ought to sound either deeply distasteful or hilariously funny.

The more students are thought of as raw material being processed into finished articles, the less they will be seen as growing human beings, with doubts, sorrows, joys, hopes and ambitions. They will be seen too much in terms of future usefulness, too little as people already living important lives. Only a few will have learnt to live with long-term deferred goals, carrying on their living outside school and using their time in it as a preparation for later life: most, especially those new fifth-formers referred to above, expect to live in the present every part as much as in the future.

In fact, the argument for granting the student some voice in the running of the school is double-edged. If they are looking to the present, then they are more likely to sense a commitment to the school if they have a share in the responsibility for it. If they are learning in school how to take their place in a democracy when they have left, then training in the procedures of representative government should start in preparation for citizenship.

Our tradition, however, has been much more one of keeping the young in their place until they have undergone the *rite de passage* of leaving for work. In our productive–consumer society, adult status is equated with employment, payment and purchasing power. Nobody has yet suggested disenfranchising the unemployed, but there are regular, vigorous and powerful voices raised against students in higher education exerting any political power at all. ('They are given their grants to study. Let them get on with it and stop passing resolutions.') How much more difficult it has been to accept the notion that the adolescent, even the sixth-former, might be allowed the dignity of contributing to the conduct of the society they belong to.

Nevertheless, a wide range of schools have experimented with some form of a school council (not to be confused with the Schools Council). Usually this has been representative of the different groupings within the student body of the school and places on it were gained by election. Some have clear constitutions, others may have very broad terms of reference. Some have teacher members so that the body is in effect a student–teacher council: others conduct their business on their own and refer direct to the Head. Almost universally, however, powers are limited to recommendation, and issues confined to domestic rather than academic or disciplinary ones.

The rock on which most school councils perish is the Head. The constantly repeated story is that the council has made recommendations on burning issues only to have them 'considered' by the Head, or to be told that responsibility for curriculum and discipline is the Head's and not within their terms of reference. The council has found itself limited to peripheral concerns such as the rules for queuing at the coffee bar, or whether to run a disco for Oxfam rather than Age Concern. Apathy then develops and the staff conclude cynically that it was a passing whim, that their students prefer to know that someone else is taking the decisions for them.

The very real possibilities of participation involving staff and students have scarcely been given the chance to prove themselves. Where they have been, it has been found to have a profound effect upon relationships within the school.[14]

It is not surprising in the light of this that even after the issue of the Taylor Report,[15] with its cautious recommendation that governing bodies should include seats not only for parents and teachers but also school students, that little has been done in this direction. The repressive reactions of the period 1975–77 put a stop to many tentative moves towards this measure of student participation. Sheffield Education Authority had before that authorised all secondary schools' governing bodies to admit student membership. Other authorities blocked any overtures on legal grounds, claiming that governors carried responsibilities in law so that a member below the age of eighteen was unthinkable. Leicestershire, formerly noted for its imaginative innovations, raised rather more obscure objections in its Education Committee, and scowled hard enough to deter its governing bodies. Which is all a great pity, since a school's students can be relied on to put forward a representative who is likely to contribute with as much restraint, relevance, good sense and discretion as the average member nominated by the local authority. And that's a bitter pill to swallow.

9. Community colleges

Chapter 7 will take up this theme more fully. In a way, there is nothing novel any longer about the *idea* of a school serving its local community, sharing its facilities. The first Village College was opened by Henry Morris, Secretary for Education, Cambridgeshire, at Sawston in 1930, and that part of the story is fairly familiar.[16] The germination of Henry Morris's idea in other parts of the country was slow. Leicestershire under Stewart Mason was the first county to follow Cambridgeshire with a complete coverage by community colleges.[17] Leicestershire's development over the period 1960–77 was a model for careful but imaginative innovation. A determined policy, to provide a county-wide service through community colleges, was carried through step by step, with patience and a visible care for the people involved. Local interests were taken into account, the proper supports tactfully enlisted. Few innovations have been so soundly constructed.

The full effect of the community college has not as yet been felt, even in Leicestershire. The early stages of the transition took up very much what Henry Morris had accomplished, which was a provision for adult interests attached to a secondary school. Even with elaborate instruments and articles of government that ensured a measure of control by representatives of the community, and even with premises used alternately by schoolchildren and adults, the earlier colleges remained schools, with the rest added on. Only recently have the boundaries, physical and psychological, between school students and adult students begun to come down.[18]

As these boundaries are removed, a number of fundamental challenges are being made to the notion of school and what it is for. Who is a student? Who is a schoolchild? How does one study? What does one study? Why does one study? When does one study? Who determines the curriculum? What restrictions may teachers reasonably place on students? What is work? What is play? Who shall we learn from? We!?

10. Alternative schools

The most significant, and scandalous, aspect of the Free School phenomenon has been that it has had to operate outside the maintained system of local education authorities. The Free Schools are in fact the opposite pole to the Public Schools, 'free' in the sense of being independent of the state system, offering a service to those for whom that system appeared not to provide a suitable education. The big difference is that the Public Schools cater for the moneyed classes who can endow them with what they want for their children, whereas the Free Schools cater for the deprived and the inadequate. Almost invariably the Free Schools have themselves remained deprived and inadequate, if not actually forced to close down, by lack of money.

The accusation that all the comprehensive schools are virtually the same flies in the face of evidence. Each has its distinctive characteristics. But, nevertheless, local authorities claim that by definition each of its comprehensives will provide full and adequate secondary education for any child (apart from the handicapped). It is this claim that seems unrealistic. There are far too many school-phobics, children who have become ill or disturbed by fear or hate of school. Much more numerous are those for whom, as I have already claimed, school fails to give any sense of satisfactory achievement but who soldier on, whether patiently or rebelliously. These are the students who are under-achieving for want of a suitable alternative.

In his useful account of the movement, *Free Way to Learning*,[19] David Head defines the 'free' of Free Schools in seven different ways. He claims that they are: (i) free from the state system; (ii) free to be a full-time alternative; (iii) free to challenge the assumptions of schooling and society; (iv) free of charge; (v) free in choices for curriculum; (vi) free to explore within the community; and (vii) free to excourage the deprived to learn ways to free themselves. I opened this section with a reference to scandal advisedly: apart obviously from David Head's first claim (to freedom from the state system) all the other six freedoms *ought* to operate equally within the maintained school system. There is no doubt, however, and I speak from bitter experience, that an introduction of any of the others will run into opposition from one quarter or more. (In a sense, secondary education is free of charge, but not to those who wish to resume where they left off after a break, and not without financial burden to sixth-formers, who sacrifice the social security payments made to their contemporaries who leave school for unemployment. There are also other hidden financial disincentives.)

There will always be *some* children for whom any school or learning programme will fail at *some* time. But these should be very few, and it still leaves a large number who are able and willing to learn, but cannot make the necessary compromises to get what they need from their neighbourhood school. Some are just too aware of the extent to which school is processing them, turning them into acceptable products. In a recent discussion with a dozen fellow secondary Heads, we agreed that the number of 'unschoolables' we encountered were fewer than 0.1 per cent of our school population. There must be, in my own estimate, as many as 5 per cent who fail at present but who would flourish in a suitable alternative setting.

No local education authority in Britain has acknowledged this to the point of offering a viable alternative. The Inner London Education Authority has 'intermediate centres' that make temporary provision for non-attenders at their schools, but their very name implies that this is a means of returning them to 'normal' full-time schooling. Liverpool paid lip-service to its Scotland Road Free School, as ILEA did to Islington's White Lion Free School, two of the best-known schools in the movement, but neither Authority was able in the end to furnish the necessary resources to keep them alive.

Poverty, low-level accommodation and the association with 'down-town' and 'underprivileged' districts has also caused the Free School alternative to be linked in the public mind, however unjustly, with social misfits and low ability. True, there can't have been many professional families that sent a child to a Free School, but still the stigma attached to the movement is unjust and unfortunate. The fact to be faced is that failed school students include very able and articulate youngsters who have run foul of the system for one reason or another. One good reason might be that they need to make rapid progress but are held back to the pace of others in their class, or the pace that is determined by insensitive teachers. Another reason might be that they have rejected the ritual values of the school and refuse to conform, thus being at loggerheads with the authorities. It is impossible even to effect a transfer to another school within the LEA supposing one might offer a better deal, unless the parent is prepared, and able, to fight the issue with determination.

It could be done. It happens elsewhere. Minneapolis, for instance, offers its parents no fewer than forty options within its High School network, each with a clearly stated bias. Elsewhere in the United States there are instances of High Schools that have been able to establish an alternative organisation on their own campus, with its own set of aims, curriculum choices and staff committed to that style. Parents and students can then opt for alternative A or alternative B of the particular school, with no stigma. There are bound to be drawbacks, naturally. Images could harden, so that A became the 'traditional' school while B became the 'progressive'. Such labelling would be restrictive to both. Nevertheless, there are less vulnerable arrangements.

The most laudable innovation in the direction of a Free School within a maintained system that I have seen personally was in Christchurch, New Zealand. Here the school authority had accepted, calmly and rationally, that a sufficient number of children ran foul of their standard High School system (13–18) to warrant an alternative provision. It was recognised that their main stumbling-block was the prevailing system of instruction, closely followed by resistance to the formalities of school as an institution. These children were identified right across the ability and social range. An approach was made to the parents concerned and as a result in 1975, a house in the centre of town was purchased as a base for a school and a Director appointed to organise it. It was called Four Avenues, taking its name from the streets that formed the boundaries of the original settlement of Christchurch. Central to the whole idea was the support won in advance by the local authority of a full range of libraries, offices, factories, workshops and so on, that would offer resources for learning to the students of Four Avenues. It opened with some eighty students, chosen by ballot from all the children whose parents had applied, is run democratically, and the staff are there to guide and co-ordinate study programmes either in the house-base or within the provision of the locality.

The lesson of Four Avenues is that where the need for an alternative provision is recognised by a local authority not as an admission of failure but as a perfectly natural course, and where the ground is carefully laid with parents and local departments and businesses, such an undertaking can be carried through with the necessary supports, success and a sense of pride.[20]

Conclusions

The purpose of this chapter has been two-fold. First, to place in juxtaposition a number of educational innovations, most of them familiar enough to teachers and education officers, but worth drawing to the notice of lay readers who may not know of them all, so as to see what lessons they may provide for innovation in general. Second, to discover any resultant direction in which they point, any spur they may provide to a qualitative advance in post-primary education.

It seems plain that within a democracy, for any major educational reform to succeed, the administration must have either created or responded to a sufficient public support for success to be assured. The campaign for this public legitimation may have to be long and persistent, as in the reform towards comprehensive schooling. In localised enterprise the preparation needs to reach a certain threshold of enthusiasm among parents and teachers likely to be affected, before the plans 'go critical' and pass the point of no return. If teachers show real conviction over a development and have the approval of their local officers and if they persist to the point of showing results that benefit the students, then parents will legitimate the approach. If, on the other hand, all parties are enthusiastic except for the teachers, an innovation will be merely a superficial rearrangement, lacking spirit and doing no good to students. Many comprehensive reorganisations have crushed individuals because teachers' attitudes had not undergone the changes necessary to ensure a human process. Efficient management is not enough.

Where right attitudes and the will to succeed have been lacking, and the theoretical aims not thoroughly thought through to the point of agreement, an innovation will founder. There is no danger that ambitious people with a little power (and every teacher has *some* power) may embark upon a new approach or display a new attitude, in order to keep up with current trends, in fear of being left behind. This danger of 'trendiness' is a pitfall for the reactionary as well as the progressive. Just now the trendy thing is to proclaim (despite the lack of sufficient evidence) that standards have fallen and that we must concentrate on drills in basic skills. Without clearly defined aims and a model of action for achieving those aims, any innovation is open to the accusation of being mere trendiness. An ill-conceived innovation of this kind, such as an attempt to set up a token school council, will not only founder, but by confirming the predictions of the doubters on hand, it will bring innovation as such into disrepute and make any future innovation the harder to launch. To embark on an innovation involving human spirit, without reasonable evidence of its viability and commitment to seeing it through to success is a grossly irresponsible abuse of power. There can be no justification for an innovation that is not expected to make some improvement, however small, to the human condition. As parents say, they don't want their children experimented with.

What have been the collective pointers in the innovations, the ones with distinguishable aims and not the ones that exemplify doing something simply because there is pressure to do something or other? Do any of them point down blind alleys? What do others point ahead to?

There seems to have been an increased awareness simultaneously of the needs of individual school students and the needs of society. In some ways this reveals an old paradox. Certainly the needs of the individual and the needs of society may conflict, but the tension between the two can be productive if each, the individual and existing society, can be seen in clearer detail.

The needs of the school student have led to a demand for equal opportunities for all and for greater attention to individual differences. These differences have not always been attended to. There are vast areas of grey uniformity in schools. But a recurrent theme has been that of diversity. Variety has been encouraged in styles of learning, materials employed, choices within the curriculum. There has been an increased awareness of variations that need to be allowed for different ripenings to occur: the 'late-developer' has become a familiar figure, and the notion of lifelong learning has begun to find currency.

At the same time, the needs of society have been expressed in new ways to the schools. The amorphous mass of school-leavers, pouring out on to the job-market, has begun to resolve into a more differentiated pattern of individuals with particular attributes searching for jobs that call increasingly for particular skills and potentials. Not all the outcomes of this have been happy. As a result, there has been a vast increase in the examinations industry to meet the call for certification from parents and employers. Not all those bits of paper are worth much. Nevertheless, within the welter of examining, emphasis has shifted, however slightly, towards assessment of work done over a period of months rather than just that done under pressure, to which many respond adversely, in the examination room.

These shifts point towards greater attention to learning rather than teaching, increased responsibility placed upon the learner to make decisions, greater co-operation between teachers and learner, between teachers and the world outside.

They will create new and heavy demands upon teachers and society, but if they are reversed or retarded, the effects upon schools could be disastrous. Meeting the new demands will entail a clear rationale for what schools are expected to do. It will entail changed roles for students, teachers and Heads. It will need still to change schools as we know them generally today beyond recognition. Where will these pointers lead us to? In the following chapters I shall examine more fully the needs of society and the student so as to find a rationale for the school of the future.

Notes

1. Most strongly recommended for clarity and accuracy:
    (a) D. Rubinstein and B. Simon, *The Evolution of the Comprehensive School 1926–1972*, Routledge and Kegan Paul, 2nd edn, 1973.
    (b) R. Pedley, *The Comprehensive School*, Penguin, 2nd edn, 1969.
    (c) C. Benn and B. Simon, *Halfway There*, Penguin, 2nd edn, 1972.
2. Hadow Report, *The Education of the Adolescent*, HMSO, 1926.
3. B. Jackson and D. Marsden, *Education and the Working Class*, Routledge and Kegan Paul, 1962.
4. As recently as 1973 the Chairman of Leicestershire Education Committee, Alderman Peter Hill, asked the staff at Countesthorpe why they wanted to treat all children the same. The staff replied with one voice, that on the contrary, they tried to treat each one differently.
5. There could be spectacular exceptions, as for instance at Crown Woods in 1960, when a fourth-year student could choose in a physical education session any of fourteen different sporting activities.
6. D. Holbrook, *English for Maturity*, Cambridge University Press, 1961; *English for the Rejected*, Cambridge University Press, 1964.
7. B. Jackson, *Streaming: An Education System in Miniature*, Routledge and Kegan Paul, 1964.
8. *Forum for the Discussion of New Trends in Education* (published three times a year). (The Manager, 11 Beacon Street, Lichfield WS13 7AA.)
9. T. Becher and S. Maclure, *The Politics of Curriculum Change*, Hutchinson, 1978.
10. The point was already made in the Newsom Report *Half Our Future* (HMSO, 1963) Ch. 10. Of the CSE it says: 'It should not be allowed to shape the whole education offered by the schools... for all the pupils a substantial part of the curriculum should be unexamined.'
11. Schools Council Working Paper 43, *School Resource Centres*, Schools Council and Evans Brothers, 1972; L. Taylor, *Resources for Learning*, Penguin, 1971; Emmeline Garnett, *Area Resource Centre: An Experiment*. Edward Arnold, 1972.

12. R. S. Peters (ed.), *The Role of the Head*, Routledge and Kegan Paul, 1976.
13. Elizabeth Richardson, *The Teacher, The School and the Task of Management*, Heinemann, 1973.
14. J. F. Watts, *The Countesthorpe Experience*, Allen and Unwin, 1977; 'Creative conflict', a paper in *A Question of Schooling*, ed. J. E. C. MacBeath, Hodder and Stoughton, 1976.
15. The Taylor Report: *A New Partnership for our Schools*, HMSO, 1977.
16. H. Ree, *Educator Extraordinary: The Life and Achievement of Henry Morris*, Longman, 1973; C. Poster, *The School and the Community*, Macmillan, 1971.
17. S. Mason (ed.), *In our Experience*, Longman, 1970.
18. An interesting comparison of the first Leicestershire community college with a recent one is made by Pauline Jones in her *Community Education in Practice – A Review*. (Published 1978 by Social Evaluation Unit, 40, Wellington Square, Oxford OX1 2JE.)
19. D. Head (ed.), *Free Way to Learning*, Penguin, 1974.
20. The story of Four Avenues is yet to be written in full, though articles have been published, notably in the *P.P.T.A. Journal of N.Z. Teachers*. The address is: Four Avenues, School Without Walls, 26 Gloucester Street, Christchurch 1, New Zealand.

4 1980–2000. The needs of society and the needs of the individual

In spite of reorganisation and new surface currents of the kind outlined in Chapter 3, little has changed at the interface of teacher and school student. The pattern in the classroom is still predominantly one of teachers deciding what their class ought to know, telling it to them and then grading them on the accuracy with which they can recall what they memorise. At its crudest, the three Rs are still rote, retention and regurgitation. In terms of content, too, little has changed. Our schools are ideal for preparing the young to take their place in a society that has already passed. We train them to leave school ready to be instant grandparents. Should we not try to turn this whole scheme of things through 180 degrees to look towards the future?

To do that is, at first sight, fraught with risk. It is so easy to come a cropper by crystal-ball gazing. So many forecasts for the near future have turned out to be ludicrous, from predicted dates for the end of the world, which have left groups naked on the mountain-top, to extrapolations of present circumstances which have then embarrassingly altered. (Like the nineteenth-century estimate that the increase of road traffic would within 100 years leave our trunk roads six feet deep in horse dung.)

Nevertheless, some degree of futurology is inescapable for the educationists, if they are to equip their young for the lives ahead of them rather than for a present that for them will be the immediate past. At most other times in the past this problem was negligible, since the conditions of the near future were usually much the same as those of the near past. Increasingly though, in our time, the rate of change has required us, like Alice and the Red Queen, to run as fast as possible just to stay where we are.

We may not know in any detail what the world will be

like in A.D. 2000, but certain features can be identified because they exist already. As Alvin Toffler summed it up – 'the Future is Now'.[1] Certain changes have already occurred that seem unlikely to be reversed. They already strain the cultural and moral norms in such ways as to have enormous significance for schools, and yet we have hardly started to take account of them. Unless we do, schooling is going to be so irrelevant to life outside that our young will scorn it. Some already do, if not precisely for this reason. What are the changes that should radically affect our thinking about future-orientated schooling? I want to raise six, in order to consider their implications.

First let us consider the increased social mobility of those whose children we teach. When I started teaching, only a quarter of a century ago, the girl in the class who went on holiday in Spain, because her father worked for the railway and had concessional travel fares, was an object of wonder. Today the odd one out would be the one holidaying at home. At that time it was possible to find individuals who had spent all their lives within a mile or two of home. Friends of mine now are incredulous when I tell them of the old lady I knew in Jersey who had never seen the sea until admitted in her eighties to the old people's home. (In Jersey the furthest point from the sea is two and a half miles.) But now everybody gets about, driving, cycling, hitching, whether in families or pairs or individually.

It is easy to scoff at the English family abroad, demanding their steak and chips, but there is no denying the increased familiarity, however superficial, with the ways of foreigners, whether from other counties or abroad – their language, customs, aspirations and settings.

Even without travel, daily exposure to television has given people an awareness of other life-styles, places and objects, that at least renders them less alarming and comic than they were even a generation ago. Of course, the rubbing off has been mutual, so that foreigners look less markedly different than they used to. But at any rate, teachers have less need now to introduce to their classrooms those colourful posters and exotic objects that formerly enlivened the lesson: they have all been seen on TV the night before, probably in colour.

Mobility has not been confined to holiday and business travel. People move about more in pursuit of their work, and now that we have gone into Europe, this may cause not only the manager to tour internationally, but the worker to take employment overseas. Children as a result become severed from grandparents and neighbourhood friends. Either the nucleus of the family becomes impacted, or the father is frequently absent.

There is not only geographical mobility and social mobility but added to this is the mobility in work. Within a lifespan, people are increasingly likely to change their occupation, retraining once, twice or more as specialist demands alter. Just as more skilled labour is needed, so is increased adaptability. The concept of training for a lifetime, that underpinned the tradition of apprenticeship, is already redundant.

People change jobs: people change partners. Friendships may often have to be less enduring. Certainly the divorce rate has rocketed. What was talked of with bated breath within the family when I was a child, is now everyday conversation. My own younger children have expressed some sense of deprivation at having to put up with the same father constantly, when so many friends had a different Dad who came to take them off to football matches or other outings on Saturdays. I am not repentant about this – shifting marriages seems to me to have mainly unsettling effects upon children. But I am forced to accept that the norm has altered.

The second change is a related one. Travel, social mobility, increased employment in distribution and servicing jobs, regular television, have all had the dual effect of diversifying and thinning human relationships. In other words, people, and their children, meet many more people, but don't really get to know them. The intensity of social intercourse has been diluted. Television viewers know of a wide range of people, fictitious and living, thrown indistinguishably together, from the Queen to Alf Garnett, so that their features are instantly recognisable. But the relationship is entirely one-sided. Everyone knows Jimmy Savile, and it is easy to believe that Jimmy Savile knows everybody. He certainly tries to give that impression. But there is no reciprocity. Sooner or later, the child becomes a man or woman, and realises that the chummy, wish-fulfilling image has little more reality than Father Christmas. Some remain with their fantasy, believe in the Archers and carry on living vicariously.

This is of course only one aspect of the way in which television interposes itself in the child's continuous construction of reality in the world he is experiencing. The screened image can become the substitute for the object beyond it. I took a twelve-year-old son to see the sights of London and ended up in Parliament Square at a red light, facing Big Ben just on the hour. It had grown dark and the face was illuminated. I wound down the window to hear the chimes, but we mostly heard traffic. The boy shrugged and said, recollecting News at Ten, 'It's not as good as the real thing.' The representation had supplanted the original.

Not only had the screen rearranged realities, it has denied the young viewer the right of reply. There is no dialogue to enter into. This can result in a real deprivation, particularly for the secondary-aged adolescent. This is essentially a period during which pressing questions of personal identity need to be answered. The child transforming into an adult, examining his own surprisingly long legs, or aware of her suddenly developing breasts, asks, 'Who am I now?' The question is answered through interactions with others, and unless these existential uncertainties are to be merely reinforced between adolescents in their own groups, the interactions must involve adults. Of course the questions are not simple and direct, and often come in the form of challenges, 'Why do this? Why say that?' But they often come back to some form of 'Who do you think I am?'

And of course, the face in the screen will not answer that question. The message, however, is either 'You are non-existent', or at best, 'You are an inarticulate but happy moron.' The adolescent who will not accept this may be driven to find identity in the peer-group, which carries the danger of identity without personal responsibility. Or, to refer again to Mia Kellmer Pringle, there may be a resort to fight or flight, aggression or withdrawal. What they desperately need are honest, trusting, working relationships, to help them establish a personal identity that will survive the lifelong shifts and rearrangements that lie ahead for them.

The adolescent struggle for individual identity is complicated by the third development I have selected. At the time when the school-leaving age has been raised, the age of onset of puberty has dropped. This means that quite apart from the appearance of sixth-form brides, we now have sixteen-year-olds in compulsory full-time education, legally entitled to marry, have children and carry legal responsibilities.[2] There has recently been a well-publicised case of a sixteen-year-old girl who married a popular professional footballer and gave up school. Her father was taken to law for failing to ensure that she returned to school. He claimed that she was no longer his responsibility but, being legally married, her husband's. The law scratched its head.

Even if they don't marry, and the case of the footballer's wife was admittedly an isolated one, they have access to contraceptives, particularly the Pill. Research findings are not yet available on the effects of this upon attitudes and attainments in school. It is none the less obvious that teachers are meeting at least a far greater knowingness about sexual practices than they used to. In my own experience this does seem to have reduced the sexual furtiveness that used to be apparent in this age-range; there is less tittering at naughty innuendos, less asking of embarrassing questions. This is not to deny that greater knowingness, greater frankness, may be accompanied by greater anguish in handling emotional entanglements. The teacher cannot avoid being aware of these entanglements between his students, and with others outside school, and if he is not wary, between his students and himself. The whole situation is further complicated by calls, even from within the legal profession, for lowering the age of consent from sixteen to fourteen.

A fourth element in present-day morality is to be associated with the vast increase in the quantity of manufactured goods available in the Western capitalist world. A cornucopia of desirable objects, hardware and consumable goods, has been spilled before our eyes, and persistent, expensively prepared advertisement has successfully whetted the public appetite for owning, using, consuming them. The advertising has deliberately endowed people with a sense of entitlement to these goods. 'You deserve them. You need them. Come and get them', is what we are constantly told. And there it is on display, within arm's reach.

The arrangement of the supermarkets, the clothes shops, the electrical goods warehouses, with everything on show, gives the appearance of Aladdin's cave. Only you have to pay. And there lies the rub. Our society is still based upon the sanctity of property. People may be more careless about their minor possessions, but they still regard them jealously as theirs. On the larger scale, the weight of the law makes it abundantly clear that property is still more sacred than personal violation: bank robbery is more punishable than rape.

Schools have had a growing problem from this simultaneous increase of personal possessions, covetousness of other people's goods and righteous possessiveness towards one's own belongings. Some of the young have consciously rejected this materialism, adopting an attitude of easy-come-easy-go. Their parents, on the other hand, have not.

My fifth example of changing attitudes in society is not particularly new, but has had a sudden increased effect in schools with the raising of the leaving age. I refer to the decline of respect for authority. The recent crisis of confidence in education would suggest that the phenomenon is the result of sloppy progressive methods in school, something directly attributable to teachers failing to exercise stricter discipline. This has been one of the themes of the Black Papers. The evidence for any general breakdown in discipline is meagre and unconvincing.[3] What is probably new and horrifying to the respectable is the extent to which disrespect is openly expressed instead of being hidden behind sham deference as it was when the lower orders could keep in the masters' good books with a touch of the cap.

Mistrust of the leadership, those who gave the orders, must date from the First World War. In most societies, authority was invested in the elders, from the *gerousia* of Sparta to the 'city fathers' of nineteenth-century municipal England. But

55

the publicly observed slaughter of this century has left the more articulate masses sceptical of those who issue the commands. After the First Battle of the Somme, young men have been less inclined to obey the order, 'Follow me, men!' than they were at the Charge of the Light Brigade. Nor were they likely to be impressed by bishops who blessed the guns. At the end of the First World War, this scepticism had become widespread – Orwell records in *The Road to Wigan Pier*: 'By 1918 everyone under forty was in a bad temper with his elders, and the mood of anti-militarism which followed naturally was extended into a general revolt against orthodoxy and authority. At that time there was, among the young, a curious cult of hatred of "old men".' It is true that in the Second World War men marched again, but not towards senseless mass slaughter, for jingoistic aims. There has been more war, but never again with crimson-coated glory and no care for 'the reason why'.

Social historians would doubtless refine this conjecture about the roots of the discredit of authority, but wherever those roots lie, and whether we regret or welcome the appearance of their fruits, the teacher, just like the works manager, can no longer expect to issue orders and be obeyed without being asked the reason why, and being required to give a satisfactory answer. For a long time, the teacher has been in a rather different position from others with authority over subordinates. He has been in charge of children. Not that children necessarily accept the command to be meek and obedient. The point is that they were smaller than their teachers and less aware of any share in adult scepticism. They could, in the last resort, and usually a good bit sooner, be thrashed into submission. Those days are past, especially since the raising of the school-leaving age, and bear little relationship to the new settings for community education. The use of violent punishment, by cane, strap, bat or hand, is a ridiculous anachronism that will have to be outlawed soon, as it has been already in every country of the Western world, in some cases for well over a century, except Britain and Ireland. A main theme of this book is the replacement of coercion, not just of corporal punishment, but that must go first.[4]

In a way, increased calls to retain or redouble the use of the cane merely reflect fear that the authority of the teacher will disappear. In Chapter 5 I shall discuss the contrast between authority and authoritarianism. There I hope to make the case that authority need not be lost if the powers of physical coercion are abandoned, and that discipline will not disappear nor be resented if it is discipline appropriate to a non-coercive style of working.

Last in this short selection of changes that already affect the society in which our schools are set, consider the explosion of knowledge. A Renaissance ideal was that of the man who knew all there was to be known. In later centuries it was still thought commendable to store in the memory all that one knew. There is still a tradition that one hears crop up among older teachers that prodigious powers of memory carry distinct advantages, particularly in examination. But we tend to hear less about 'the walking encyclopaedia' today, because the encyclopaedia has simply boiled over. Research, and rapid worldwide communications between researchers, has led to astronomic increases in what is known about the physical universe. Not only is there much more to know within every recognised subject, but each subject has sub-divided and totally new areas of knowledge have come into existence. A microbiologist may have a lifetime's enquiry ahead of him within his own field. A sedimentary geologist might find it a full-time task just to read and absorb the new information published monthly in his sub-division of the subject. It is impossible for any individual to keep abreast of what is known.

This is not confined to the higher realms of learning. Within the school it is not just the A-Level studies that are affected. New subjects make their appearance – computer studies and control technology may be taken at O-Level. More particularly, the teacher can no longer safely predict what information needs to be known in any subject in order to equip his students for life after school.

Of course it goes without saying that there is a body of

basic knowledge, associated particularly with literacy and numeracy, that every child needs to acquire, and schools cannot evade their responsibility in that respect. But even to start infant and primary schooling on a process of swallowing facts would be treacherous to the young mind. And the mastery of basic skills such as reading, writing, addition, subtraction and multiplication should be complete before secondary schooling. Even where it is not, and remedial action is called for, it would be entirely mistaken to use that as the model approach for post-primary education.

We used to be able to think of the curriculum in terms of the total of necessary knowledge divided up into subjects, each subject sub-divided into syllabuses that mapped out the route in a sequence of parcels of knowledge. The lessons would be the means by which these doses of knowledge would be transmitted to the pupil, and the examinations the means of testing whether it had gone in. It has not changed much in essence since Mr Gradgrind went to check whether the teacher in his school was teaching the facts properly.[5] The problem now is that the teacher who wants to fit his students for the future, aware of the obsolescence of syllabuses has no guide to what will be relevant, and if he considers the rate of increase of knowledge it is obvious that information not yet formulated will be needed in their lives. If he still sees his task as one primarily of transmitting information, his mind will boggle.

The implications for school are enormous and for the most part are being evaded.

These six shifts are not the only ones. Others, such as the altered ethics of work and leisure, spring to mind. But they represent social directions not likely to be speedily reversed. Nobody can predict the particular events of the future, but it is safe to say that those changes already with us are now adding to the general shape of the next quarter of a century. Even judging by these features alone, it should be clear that the young are inheriting a society that will impose great strain on them. Rates of change are continuing to increase, adaptability will be a prime requirement. These are the particular strains that civilisation imposes on our time.

I am going on to argue in Chapter 6 for altered roles to be played by all partners in education. These roles seem to me to be those that could be placed in an increasingly open form of schooling. Such openness, described in theoretical terms in Chapter 5, is a direct response to the demands and strains already outlined. These strains may now be taking new forms, but civilisation has always imposed strains on the individual once his back has turned upon tribalism. My lead here, obviously, is Sir Karl Popper. His classic account of man's unfinished struggle to advance from closed societies towards an open society emphasises the strain imposed. This strain, he writes,

> is still felt even in our day, especially in times of social change. It is the strain created by the effort which life in an open and partially abstract society continually demands from us – by the endeavour to be rational, to forge at least some of our emotional social needs, to look after ourselves, and to accept responsibilities. We must, I believe, bear this strain as the price to be paid for every increase in knowledge, in reasonableness, in co-operation and in mutual help, and consequences in our chances of survival. It is the price we have to pay for being human.[6]

The implications seem clear. The greater the pace of change, the greater the strain upon the individual and the greater the temptation to avoid reasonableness, responsibilities, co-operativeness, to lapse into the emotional comfort of tribalism. The attractive, atavistic force of tribalism, coming from the extremes of the political left and right, has been all too evident in our time. Whether in a fascist ant-hill or a soviet beehive men and women give up their freedoms and responsibilities to either the leadership or the collective.

Erich Fromm has shown how readily individuals who have regressed psychologically will avoid responsibility for solving their own problems and initiating their own actions, by seeking a Magic Helper.[7] The Magic Helper is the person or 'the cause' by whom or by which the individual arrested in this way seeks to fulfil aspirations. Fromm says the reason for anyone adopting this kind of fixation is 'an inability to stand alone and to fully express his own individual potentialities'. He goes on to identify authoritarianism and its personifications as the most attractive Magic Helper. Recourse to invoking the Magic Helper is heard in the cry 'Tell me what to do', with the implication '. . . and I'll do it'.

Subservience to authoritarianism, the abdication of personal responsibility, the loss of freedom, are the major threats to the individual in the society of A.D. 2000. The defence against them must require a combined knowledge of and confidence in self-identity, a readiness to face the unknown without fear, a capacity for identifying and solving new and unheralded problems, an ability to collaborate by handling the interaction of the self and others. All this points to an urgent need for a society of individuals who can shape their own destinies with less reliance than in the past from precedent, tradition and dogma.[8] No list of basic skills in our time can overlook these basics for survival.

Schools will not save society, but they can either help or hinder. If they are so designed as to foster these abilities, they will make the survival of the individual and a free society more likely rather than less so, they will prepare individuals to modify and shape the world they move into and inherit. None of the changes described so far has gone far enough to redesign schools so that they meet this challenge. We may advocate individual responsibility and enterprise, but our rewards still go to the conformist, in school as outside it. What pays off most rapidly is conformity to the opinions, attitudes and expectations of those within the authority structure. It is time that we practised what we preach.

Notes

1. A. Toffler, *Future Shock*, Random House, 1970.
2. At present a girl whose sixteenth birthday fell on 1 September would be legally bound to attend school full-time until Easter of the following year.
3. The hollowness of the accusations about indiscipline is exposed in Chapter 6 of Nigel Wright's *Progress in Education*, Croom Helm, 1977, pp. 111–23.

4. A good review of the whole question of corporal punishment is contained in P. Newell, *A Last Resort*, Penguin, 1972.

5. Charles Dickens, *Hard Times*, Ch. 1, is still compulsory reading for anyone studying the conflict between education of the human spirit and fact-grinding.

6. K. Popper, *The Open Society and its Enemies*, Routledge and Kegan Paul, 1945, Vol. 1, p. 176.

7. E. Fromm, *The Fear of Freedom*, Routledge and Kegan Paul, 1942, p. 151; see also E. Fromm, *The Sane Society*, Routledge and Kegan Paul, 1956.

8. In using this expression regularly, I acknowledge its source in an article by Derek Morrell, 'Happiness is not a meal ticket', in *The Times Educational Supplement*, 9 Dec. 1969.

5 Closed schools and open schools

In the Chapter 4 I pointed to a selection of the features that identify what Popper has described as an increasingly 'abstract' society, that is, a society whose marks of identification, habits, customs, values and membership are changing with increasing speed. This can be met by attempts to *close* our society, to appeal increasingly to the past, to hand over individual freedom and responsibility to authorities, or it can be met in an *open* society by taking the reins firmly in hand, driving into the unknown and accepting responsibility for shaping it. If the first course is adopted, if we are to retreat into a more tribal, authoritarian way of life, then our children will be better served in schools that are themselves 'closed', reflecting and preparing them for a relatively closed society: if the second course is adopted, our future and our children will be better prepared in 'open' schools, for a relatively open society.

It might be argued that this decision of public will hangs in the balance at present. This is to a considerable degree true. We live in a time of political vacillation, of leadership dither. That being so, our devil's advocate might continue, should we not suspend innovation in school and, while in doubt, carry on as before, using the tried and trusted methods? My answer is that that is itself a choice to support the first course, a rejection of the future, of openness. We cannot escape the choice. We must ask ourselves what we want for our children, starting not with other people's children (for whom it is always easier to prescribe limited options in life), but in our own families. Do we want for their adult life the security of strong authority and limited responsibility, or the dangerous threats of the unknown and responsibility for resolving them in freedom? The choice may be agonising, but that is the price of parenthood, of any advance in civilisation.

Security has its price too, and offers no guarantee of success. My own hope is for an open society of the future for my immediate family and descendants. This book is therefore an advocacy for open schooling.

In practice, we are not going to see any such early revolution of attitudes or deployment of resources in our nation as will produce a totally new system of open schools. The issue will be one of whether this or that school is relatively open or closed, which direction it is moving in and what the general trend is in schools across the country. What then are the identification marks of openness and its opposite in a school?

To answer this, I have applied to my own experience of schools a theoretical analysis that owes a lot to Bernstein.[1] I have selected ten aspects of school, as an organised society, which distinguish the open school from the closed. I have then looked for contrasts of operation and attitude in each. It may then be asked of a given school, what do we notice about each of these ten features? Suppose each of them to cover a spectrum of practice, 'open' at one end and 'closed' at the other, where do we place the school along that continuum? Or, if there have been changes along the spectrum, in which direction has the movement been? The ten elements are:

1. The establishment of values.
2. The communication and handling of criticism.
3. Authority and the exercise of control.
4. Hierarchy, structure and status.
5. The status of knowledge.
6. Teaching and learning.
7. Perceptions of reality.
8. Mutuality and study.
9. Sub-grouping.
10. Response to challenge.

1. The establishment of values

Every school will value certain things above others, whether it is chemistry above cookery or a quiet life above trouble. Individuals, with their varying degrees of authority within the school, will hold values, and between these individuals, allowing for disagreement and self-contradiction, there will be a summary of values. These may be said to be the values by which the school operates. They may be identical with the stated aims of the Head and governors, or there may be a degree of discrepancy, sometimes wide, between stated aims and operational aims.

These differences may appear in an open school as well as a closed one. However, the distinction between the two types of school is noticeable in differences over the extent to which their value systems are proclaimed. Some schools never state their aims. This could be because the Head and staff are not able to formulate them or are not interested in doing so. More often, it is because the aims and values are seen to be embodied in the traditional practices of the school and stating them would seem to be superfluous, stating the obvious. What is likely to happen then is that the values will be celebrated in ritual. The more closed a school is, the more its value system will be transmitted by ritual: the more open a school is, the more its values will be made explicit.

Ritual in school is sometimes obvious, as in ceremonies such as morning assembly, speech days or other grand occasions. The value of academic and social authority will then be symbolised by such means as robes, by the use of the platform to elevate one party and subordinate the other. These means can be used to equate academic and civic authority, as when the mayor is present wearing his chain of office, or clerical authority, when the Church's representative joins the platform party wearing some distinctive garb, if only the dog-collar, as part of his public clothing. Other, more permanent, ritual expressions of values, may be seen in the positioning of honours boards, trophy cabinets, even notice boards.

There are everyday embodiments of the staff's priorities which are no less effective and taken for granted because of their familiarity. These include styles of dress (both what is prescribed for school students and what is expected of teachers), modes of addressing one another, tones of voice, reservation of certain parts of the building as private. (The approach to the Head's room at Crown Woods used to be known as 'God's corridor'.) Beating is a ritual assertion of power and can to some degree be effective as such, though seldom as the deterrent it is made out to be if a justification is called for.

The common feature of these rituals is that they have no explicit accompaniment. They do not need to be explained in order to have their effect. One piece of the ritual code may be unintelligible, but cumulatively it carries its message in itself. There is no need for the Head to explain to those who are below *why* he is on a platform. It is self-explanatory. And therein rests the effectiveness of rituals. They are not open to question. As a consequence they are seldom likely to be altered and then only by the officiators, not by the congregation, the pupils or the novices.

Ritual is highly effective, therefore, in the transmission of values in a static situation and where there is a sufficient congruity of expectation between all the participants. Where there is too little in common between the teacher and pupil, the ritual will lose its meaning. When I went to school I did not need to know the precise origin of my teachers' gowns and colourful hoods when they wore them. I knew they symbolised academic excellence and set them aside in glory from us duller mortals as examples of the heights to which they and our parents hoped we would aspire. But when as a young teacher in a time of greater change I myself wore hood and gown as part of my Head's ritual daily service, I was asked by a puzzled girl – 'Why do some of you teachers wear them overalls in assembly?' That ritual had become meaningless, at least for her, though I suspect she was not alone in her posing of the question.

The anecdote illustrates the way in which questioning of ritual leads to its redundancy. If the question remains unanswered, the ritual becomes meaningless or at best quaint and colourful, while at worst, and in school more probably, it becomes absurd. To be effective, it must overawe. Once the pupil laughs at the ritual, it has become counter-productive.

If the teacher then retains his ritual, he retreats into indignation and thence into personal absurdity. It is not uncommon in times of change to find a teacher whose ritual is questioned, and who will not or cannot come into the open with an explanation, suffering anguish and complaining of lack of respect.

The more the teacher is ready to explain the reasons for what he does or expects of others, the more he is prepared to justify his aims and values, then the more his mode of operation may be described as open. It has nothing to do with whether he wears a collar and tie or a beard and turtle-neck. Either may be an unquestioned symbol of values being transmitted, the instrument of a hidden curriculum. What is significant is whether he is able to justify his neckwear if challenged. A school may abandon old rituals because they do not express the values that are held by its staff, but if new styles are adopted to convey messages that themselves remain unstated, then that school, perhaps deceptively informal, will be to that degree closed.

2. The communication and handling of criticism

The inadequacy of ritual in times of relatively intensive change results from the impossibility of anyone but a high authority altering it. It can only be entered into or rejected. If the teacher wishes to offer his values for adoption by his pupils, then he has to be prepared to lay them open to modification. In a closed institution, criticism is unacceptable. ('This is the way it has always been done. Yours not to reason why. This is the way you will do it.') Ritual is essentially coercive. In an open relationship there has to be a dialogue.

This dialogue is more than a matter of words. Thousands of words may be expended by teachers without their being any more open, if their main burden is to inform. It is not enough to *tell* pupils, parents and public what you are doing. To be open means entering into exchanges with all those parties with a readiness to listen as well as to talk. It means being prepared to justify one's actions in the face of criticism, or to modify practice if the justification cannot be given. Such openness is very stressful to the school, of course. Parents and pupils have for so long associated teachers with closed institutions that first signs of openness to criticism are met initially with incredulity, then with often long-delayed retaliation. Many people harbour old pent-up hostilities towards unassailable teachers and schools. When the drawbridge is first lowered and the portcullis raised, the besieging troops will rush in with swords drawn. It takes time and nerve for a peaceful two-way traffic to establish itself. But the teacher is the one who must take the first step down from his daïs, out from behind his desk (two pieces of ritual furniture), to sit around the table, preferably circular (another, but justifiable, symbolic article), and hold a conversation with parents, pupils, neighbours, if he is really to lay himself open and expect them to be open in return.

3. Authority and the exercise of control

A closed institution will tend to be controlled by specific rules. The extreme example of this would be a prison, where every aspect of daily life will be rule-governed. In the Army, Queen's Regulations are compendious, drawn up to determine action to be taken in any foreseeable circumstance.[2] The more a school is rule-governed, the more safely we may describe it as closed: the more a school is governed by specific rational agreements, the nearer it is to being open.

In the closed school, rules will be formulated by the Head, as supreme authority. He may strengthen his position by having his rules ratified by the governing body, but if he has their confidence there is hardly need for this as governors by their articles delegate to the Head 'control of the internal organisation, management, and discipline of the school'. The Head is further bound by articles which require that all proposals and reports affecting the conduct and curriculum of the school shall be submitted formally to the governors. The Head therefore has authority to draw up and apply rules without any consultation with those, his staff and students, to whom they apply. This authority is coupled with powers to reward and punish in order to maintain conduct conforming to the rules. This is what the term 'discipline' is most commonly taken to mean: the standard to which clear and sensible rules are issued and complied with.

The advantage of such a regime is that it reduces confusion about who is meant to do what in given circumstances. It avoids deviation and hesitancy. It is ideal for an organisation that has to take swift and efficient action as one body; the Army, or a unit within it, is an example. A school that is bounded by efficiently applied rules will have a discipline that guarantees, for instance, efficiently organised speech days, or well-conducted examination arrangements.

The disadvantage is that exhaustive rules are designed to tell people what to do with the minimum of uncertainty or exercise of judgement. This is a poor way to train anybody to apply basic principles to new or unforeseen situations. The subject in a rule-dominated kingdom is not likely to adjust easily to a free society, or one where the rules are few and he needs to make decisions governed by his own judgements. This is one reason why offenders tend to return to prison: the longer they spend there, the more dependent they become on it and the way it relieves them of the responsibility and strain of making decisions. Closed schools similarly prepare their pupils to operate best in a closed society, which may be why the Public Schools used to produce so many Regular Army officers. A closed school does not serve so well the leaver who moves into the changing circumstances of a relatively open society.

The operation through given rules in a society is authoritarian. Like rituals, they cannot easily be modified or rescinded, except by whoever issued them. The only reason forthcoming if an authoritarian rule is challenged is the one that says – 'Because you have to', or, 'Because I say so.' (Another classic answer I remember when asking why, was – 'To make silly boys ask questions.')

Some see the alternative to authoritarianism in anarchy, no rule. And indeed one possible form of open society would be one where no one had power over anyone else and each individual took the decisions governing his own conduct rationally, considerately and responsibly. Life on Tristan da Cunha must have been a bit like that – though it made interactions such as football matches difficult.

More practically, a society, if not that of a very small island, needs a discipline that governs conduct in order to achieve cohesion and survival. How is this possible in an open society or open school? I would offer again the criterion of degree to which the common member may challenge or modify a rule. The greater this possibility, the more the government is by consent. Mechanisms of reaching the consent are necessary and will no doubt vary, but it is fair to call a school relatively open once a way of achieving and enforcing consensus is reached.

A stated rule may at times be identical in an open or closed school. For instance, any school may have the rule: No Smoking in Toilets. The significant differences will be in how it was made, how it is enforced and how it may be changed or rescinded. In a closed school, the rule will be issued with the authority of the Head, who will be empowered to punish infringement. In an open school, the rule will have been agreed by consensus among the members (all those to whom the rule applies, staff and students): infringement will be curbed by action, possibly punitive, by the same consensual arrangement. The authority is still present, but it is shared, agreed to and open to modification. It is effective when and where those affected accept the ruling of their peers, because in those circumstances there is more likelihood of willing compliance rather than conformity under duress.

It is worth mentioning one last characteristic of discipline and authority in an open school. There need to be only few specific rules. The expectation is that individuals will act increasingly by reason on basic principle, as a result of becoming accustomed to agreements that are reached by discussion. In other words, the individual's expertise will become that of making an *adhoc* rule for himself, internally, in answer to the question, 'What should I do?' In a closed society, the expertise is in knowing the rules. It tends to produce barrack-room lawyers, and their prolonged disputes turn not on what is reasonable, but on interpretation, to their own advantage, of the complex rules.

It goes without saying that only a relatively closed institution can enforce rules that are unwelcome to the majority. A good indicator is prescribed uniform dress. In spite of claims that school students actually like having a uniform, I think it safe to claim that where the decision is genuinely one by consensus among those affected, choice of clothing would never be left to a single authority.

4. Hierarchy, structure and status

In many schools still, the staffroom will contain certain privileged chairs reserved by unwritten rule for individual senior teachers. Woe betide the presumptuous probationer who sits in one of them. This is typical of the minor privilege that serves to indicate how much importance the school attaches to rank. A school that causes deference to rank is relatively closed: a school that encourages deference to individual performance and weight of reason, is relatively open. In a closed school, the junior will give way to his senior's opinion regardless of the strength of its supports. This will work up the ladder of seniority so that what the Head finally has to say will decide any issue.

Such a strong chain of seniority forms a clear hierarchy that will leave the junior teacher in a position where he has little chance of prevailing in any conflict. He has to exercise his seniority in turn over his students. It has been shown that the stronger the hierarchy is in any organisation, the more difficult it is to communicate in an upwards direction, for the junior to get the ear of the principal.[3] By the same token, communication of information and directive is relatively easy from the top downwards. In a hierarchical structure, therefore, change is likely to be initiated only from the top. This means that change is most likely to occur with the appointment of a new Head: the longer a Head has been in office, the less likely is he either to want change or to have the fresh ideas that would be needed. The consequence is that in stable times a hierarchical organisation may persist, but when change is rapid, either new leadership is drafted in, or the hierarchy will be shaken up from below. This happens to peacetime armies: between wars their hierarchy tends to be static, but in war the outcome may well be decided by whichever side can most effectively give opportunities to its young recruited officers, what used to be called 'temporary gentlemen' in the First World War.

So in a closed school, status is assigned, albeit initially on merit, but so that rank carries an authority which is then distinct from either competence or logic. It would be hoped that a holder of senior rank would continue to display competence and good reasoning power, but even when those capacities are not evident, he remains after all, the head of department, or whatever, and that still counts. In an open school, status would tend to be acquired in the eyes of others on continued merit in performance. If performance fell off, the expectation would be for a change of status and function. This would be unthinkable in a closed school.

The concept of rank with a clearly defined order of command inevitably spreads in a closed school from staff to students. There, too, a distinct pecking order will develop. The indicators of a closed school in this respect will be the existence of class monitors, year and house captains, prefects, senior prefects, head student. These will be distinguished by badges, other marks of dress, deportment and speech even, as one approaches the pinnacle. The concept of rank can become so much part of the accepted order in closed schools that it seems natural to have rank order in each class, a rank order in each year, and each year regarded as one step higher, not just in age, but in seniority. The scheme will be divisive and progress for the individual will be accomplished by conformity and time.

The more open is the school, the more fluid the divisions between ranks will become. Excellence will tend to be judged on particular performance, not summed up and associated with rank. Movement between positions will be easy, for student or staff. In a closed school, resistance to say, a fourth-year student studying for some periods with the sixth form, or a head of department teaching a junior remedial class, will arise not so much on rational, pragmatic grounds (though obstacles may be raised on such grounds) but in a vaguer way because it doesn't seem right. It would damage the neat balance of the hierarchical structure.

5. The status of knowledge

What I am concerned to draw attention to in this section is the extent to which the staff of a school view knowledge as something existing in its own right, which they have to get inside their students. I have already raised the problem of defining what basic common core of knowledge we may expect our children to possess. I have also mentioned the increasing difficulty, especially in post-primary education, of selecting from the huge and expanding body of knowledge, those items it might be thought necessary to transmit to school students. My interest here, though, is the positioning of teachers upon that continuum at one end of which knowledge is seen as facts to be transmitted, and at the other as what the individual has learnt as a result of exploratory encounters with the world about him. The position will further help to describe the degree to which their school is open or closed.

The teacher adopting an authoritarian position will envisage knowledge as a compendium of information which either he possesses, within himself, or has the key to. In either case, he controls knowledge and its distribution. In this position, the teacher can donate to his students what they need to know in return for the right responses. He may use his imagination, his personal charm and a battery of professional techniques to make his lessons attractive, interesting and effective. But if his aim is to transmit what is already known by himself and others to the ignorant, then his view of knowledge is characteristic of a closed school.

If, on the other hand, he sees knowledge as what the student acquires in course of exploration, his approach will differ. His task will then consist of putting his students in the track of experiences from which they may acquire knowledge, by stimulating interest, supplying the right resources and providing the necessary skills. In this way, the student's knowledge will be his own, acquired and not donated by an owner.

The closed view of knowledge, as something transferable, enhances the importance of examination since knowledge, seen this way, is something that lends itself to checking. If you have been handed it by the teacher, you may also hand it back. The open view of knowledge recognises it as something 'far more deeply interfused' with the knower, something which, to be meaningful, will have become an integral part of the learner, and can never be fully surrendered in an examination.

6. Teaching and learning

The implication for schools of the explosive growth of human knowledge has been that the teacher cannot possibly select, possess and transmit what on prediction his students are going to need to know in life. The closed view is appropriate in a time of static knowledge and immobile society. In a period of expansion and change, the emphasis shifts in an open response away from the content of *what* is taught, towards *how* the student may learn. If the problems of the future cannot be predicted, then it is crucial that the student learns in school: (a) how to identify a problem (whereas in a closed class the problem is always posed by the teacher); (b) how to plan a strategy for solving the problem (instead of teacher detailing the method); (c) how to select and retrieve the information necessary for this problem-solving strategy; (d) how to derive hypotheses from this data – i.e. logical processes; (e) how to test hypotheses. In an open approach, the teacher will be concerned to promote those skills rather than supply information. He will be concerned with how his student goes about his problem-solving and is less preoccupied than his closed colleague with being given the right answer.[4]

Given the open approach, the teacher will also encourage

imaginative speculation. Outside schools, problem-solving involves a lot of trial and error, intelligent guesswork and 'story-telling'.[5] This will lead to extensive talk, of a kind that will have little to do with conveying information, and a lot to do with considering alternatives. It will be full of expressions like 'Why not. . .' and 'What if. . .' or 'Just suppose. . .'. It will be noisier than study is supposed to be, and much more playful. In fact it confuses work and play in ways quite outrageous to the closed schoolroom.

7. Perceptions of reality

From what has gone before it is clear that learning in an open school is a process by which the student arrives at conclusions about the world which derive from his own endeavours and experience. In this way, piecemeal, he will construct and reconstruct his reality, in terms of a series of interactions between himself and the world. It is a course in which the student is also constructing his own sense of identity. The interactions occur as much between the student and his surrounding society as between him and physical events.[6]

In a closed school, the approach to learning, the conception of knowledge as an enclosed bank or repository to which the student may be given limited admission, the use of knowledge indeed as a means of controlling the student,[7] all suppose a view of reality as something maintained by an authority and transmitted to a learner who remains passive, 'like a patient etherised upon the table'.

8. Mutuality and study

If the teacher is conveying knowledge to his students *de haut en bas*, then their relationship is aptly symbolised by the master's raised dais and the student's bench below. (The belief that the teacher is dropping pearls before swine was strong enough for one of my teachers when I was a boy to cause him to order us each to label his notebook with the word 'trough'.) In a closed school there is no room for the teacher to learn from the student. The very idea will be repugnant to the authoritarian teacher, except in stray examples of odd and unimportant information. So powerful can this faith in his own infallibility become for the closed teacher, that he will find it hard to admit to ignorance on any point and will resort to dodges if detected in any apparent error. ('I made that mistake deliberately to see if any of you would be bright enough to spot it.')

The teacher in an open school has no need to pretend that he knows all the answers, or even all the questions. Of course he has to be knowledgeable and resourceful, capable of testing validity, skilled at when to intervene, when to encourage, when to cut losses. But he is essentially engaged in the same pursuit of knowledge as his students. For him the apt classroom furniture is the round table. His age and experience inevitably mean that he will previously have covered a lot of the ground that his students find fresh. Nevertheless, there will be a reciprocity of interest and concern over outcome in an open school classroom. The teacher will embody this interest in the unknown.

Schools have traditionally increased motivation to learn by pitting students in competition, each against the others. For many adults, the thought of school is inseparable from comparative gradings, the publication of orders of merit, the award of public honour for the more successful, a sense of failure for the others. It has been said that competition is natural and should therefore be exploited to promote excellence and the best in others. (It is overlooked that other 'natural' tendencies, such as gluttony, avarice and sexual lust, need to be curbed.) The major drawback with competition in school is that for every winner there is a loser, and if everyone is struggling to be top of the class, for every winner everyone else is to some degree or other a loser. Life is not like that outside school. We judge each other by innumerable qualities and only very few are total failures, failures at everything. But school has traditionally managed to leave most people with a memory of failure.

There is no need for this. In a more open arrangement,

competition is replaced by co-operation. Learning need in no way be at anyone else's expense. Indeed a valuable aspect of learning is learning to help others learn. The fast readers may help the slow readers instead of making them feel inferior. In solving problems in class, just as we must often do out of school, the best strategy is usually devised by a group. There is obviously need for study and learning in isolation as well, but the teacher in an open school will devise situations that may best be resolved by students in collaboration with each other. The place for competition is the games field.

Such a mutual approach to study has radical implications for the relationships between teacher and student. There can be considerable confusion for student and school as a whole if there is an incongruity between the relative openness of one classroom and the prevailing ethos of the school. I shall explore more fully in the next chapter what changes are entailed in the relationships of an open school. It is enough here to say that studying alongside a student, leading his enquiry but remaining open to a whole range of possible outcomes, cannot co-exist with authoritarian practices in other directions. A discipline has to be found that is appropriate to the nature of the study.

9. Sub-grouping

I have already pointed out how a closed school will have a permanent structure, or hierarchy, that accords increased power the nearer the summit is approached. Sub-committees and working parties within such a framework will tend to be established by the Head, to whom they will be ultimately responsible, and membership will be by appointment from above. Examples of such sub-groups are, heads of department committees or an examinations committee. In the same way, allocation of students to their sub-groups, the classes or sets, will be made from above with limited options. This is another example of what is taken as the natural order.

The more open the school, however, the more likely it

is that sub-grouping will become autonomous. Among staff, a committee or working-party will be formed according to the task to be performed and with membership either of volunteer interested parties or on the recommendation or election by peers. It is also to be expected that such a group will disband when its particular purpose has been served. Some permanent tasks might be performed by committees in rotation. These would form what might therefore be termed 'mutable structures'.

There is no fundamental reason for study groupings of students to be any more permanent than is necessary for a sense of stability. Students are conditioned to accept that they go to school and are placed in classes determined by some mysterious and unquestioned authority. Parents are made to feel this too, so that requests for regrouping may be few. But it is perfectly possible so to arrange school as to allow great flexibility of grouping. An open school would allow any forming of groups that did not result in damage or disruption, with students free to study subjects of their own choice, attached to teachers of their choice, in company of fellow students of their own choice. Or at least it would carry that as an ideal with restrictions that resulted only from the limitations imposed by the practicalities of time and space.

Further in towards the centre of this continuum we might find more permanence in groups, but with a degree of openness that allowed membership to be heterogeneous, with some ease of transfer. This would identify unstreamed classes, each with a mixture of abilities. Moving further towards a closed arrangement, classes would be homogeneous and stratified into streams with a rank order.

10. Response to challenge

There is no reason to think that challenge in school need only be presented through competition between students or between one school and another. Except on the games field, challenge does not necessarily mean that some win only by others losing. In terms of learning, of overcoming difficulties, of resolving problems, it is possible for everybody to win.

If everybody won, whatever effort or lack of it they showed, there would be complacency and apathy. That would be Lewis Carroll's 'caucus race' where everybody got a prize. If you are going to race, race. But the alternative presented in an open school is more analogous to rock-climbing, where everybody is expected to reach the cliff-top, regardless of who gets there first, and if anyone fails to get there, everyone has failed.

In the rock-climbing analogy, learning which is mutually supportive, removing neurotic fear of failure, enables everybody to feel that they can meet the challenge of the unknown.

There always needs to be the challenge. The psychologist Richard Jones has provided a valuable account of how learning comes about.[8] He claims that three prerequisites are necessary for learning to occur: security, competence and threat. Since 'threat' suggests physical force, I prefer to use 'challenge'. If any one of these three is absent, learning will not occur. If insecurity exists instead of security, or if competence is lacking, then challenge produces instead a neurotic response, anxiety and inactivity, or irrelevant activity.

I find this helpful. It confirms first that a child needs to be happy and assured at school. It further confirms that this is not enough to ensure learning; there needs to be skill learnt from the teacher. Even this is not enough: the teacher cannot rest content with making his student happy and teaching skills. He must provide challenge.

And of course, the greatest challenge is afforded by the unknown, the open-ended problem such as life itself has increasingly become. The open school can above all offer the challenge of the unknown in a context of security (since it is open to everyone to succeed) and competence.

Notes

1. B. Bernstein, 'Open schools, open society?', *New Society*, 14 Sept. 1967, 351–3; B. Bernstein, H. L. Elvin and R. S. Peters, 'Ritual in education', *Philosophical Transactions of the Royal Society of London*

(B), 1966, 251(772), 429–36.

2. A useful reference, comparing the social situation of mental hospitals, the armed services, prisons, monastic orders and boarding schools is Erving Goffman's *Asylums*, Anchor Books, 1961; Penguin edn, 1968. It is worth noting that all of these can be 'total' institutions, completely closed in a way no day school can be.

3. D. E. Griffiths (ed.), *Behavioural Science and Educational Administration*, (63rd Year book of the National Society for the Study of Education), University of Chicago Press, 1964.

4. The bugbear of the Right Answer is exposed in John Holt, *How Children Fail*, Dell Publishing Co., 1964.

5. P. Medawar, *The Art of the Soluble*, Penguin, 1969. In these essays, Sir Peter Medawar, a Nobel prize-winner reveals how the language used by scientists in their work differs from that used when recording their findings.

6. Behind this blunt assertion looms the work of social scientists such as G. H. Mead and philosophers such as Suzanne Langer.

7. M. F. D. Young, *Knowledge and Control*, Collier-Macmillan, 1972.

8. R. M. Jones, *Fantasy and Feeling in Education*, New York University Press, 1968.

6 New schools – new roles

I have argued that our schools are still relatively closed. As they become more open, altered roles need to be taken up by all involved, teachers, Heads, students, parents, governors. Indeed, the limits of a school's openness will be virtually determined by the extent to which these people can adopt new roles for themselves. The foregoing chapters hold certain implications for these roles. A closer account of them may help to map out the course of changes ahead if we are to have schools that look to the future rather than the past. It will also indicate the strains that such demands will set up and pose the question of what those affected may expect in return.

The teacher

Take first the role of the teacher in an open school. He will above all, have to become less authoritarian, more prepared to be rational, to justify or modify. In practice, this means showing a readiness to reply patiently to the infuriating questioning by students of one's advice on learning tasks or conduct. 'Why do we have to do this? Why that way?' Only a saint will avoid replying occasionally, 'Because I say so', or 'I'll tell you why later'. But the point is that such impatient replies will be the exceptions to the rule.

The problem is complicated by British teachers having a tradition of pontificating not just on studies, but on every aspect of life. It should be laughable to think that a headmistress addressing her assembled parents should tell them what time they ought to send their children to bed. It is of course, all too common. We tell them what they should wear, what they should eat, whether they speak 'properly' or not, when they can go to the pictures. Our social presumption has been colossal and our own assumed virtues ludicrous.

Such a shift would in practice mean that teachers should stop laying down the law on social habits except where they obstruct learning. For instance, a teacher in science could justify on the grounds of safety a requirement that students should not wear overcoats in the laboratory, but since the colour of the coat is beside the point, he has no justification for prescribing that it be any particular shade or hue. A rule would need to be laid down in workshops that long hair be tied back in case it caught in machinery, but that is no reason for enforcing short haircuts on all. Yet the most enormous battles have been fought over the exact colour of socks or the precise length of hair. Whatever the ostensible reasons given by teachers and heads for this kind of purely social legislation on their part, the issue has almost invariably been that of symbolised authority and its enforcement: the defence has not finally been based on hygiene or safety, but discipline. The rule was designed to maintain the domination by master over subject. It is significant that, whatever tactical victories the schools may have won, in the long run they have retreated and lost-fashion has always prevailed, and after all who are teachers to set themselves up as arbiters of fashion?

The teacher is therefore going to be expected not only to pontificate less, to be ready to modify his practice, but to be more accessible to his students in order that this process may happen. The open school will shift the emphasis from what and how the teacher teaches to what and how the learner learns. The student will be encouraged to organise his enquiries with all the possible resources for learning. There seems little doubt that in secondary schooling the most important resource for learning is still going to be the teacher. He will be asked unpredictable, and predictable, questions which either call for information or evaluation, suggestions on procedure or encouragement and affirmation. He is not required to be a walking, talking encyclopaedia: he needs to be a person and as such he needs to be (*a*) accessible, and (*b*) open to expressive exchange.

To be accessible, teachers just need to share more time

with their students, to drop the formal barriers that we have erected as part of our traditional rituals of separateness, and now too easily take for granted. We need to abandon the ritual arrangements for separate staff and student cloakrooms, rest-rooms, refreshments, meals. The open school will abolish the staffroom, into which we so easily retreat between lessons, erecting elaborate formalities to preserve the privacy. ('Pupils may not knock at the staffroom door unless accompanied by a prefect.') The difficulties of communicating across the genera-tion gap are almost entirely of adult making. If we have faith in our own values, we should be prepared to put them to the test in moment-by-moment contact with the young.

So, having come out from behind the barrier of the staff-room door, the teacher has also to drop the personal barriers to contact with his students. By tradition, teachers have demanded middle-class formalities of approach that have, not surprisingly, made them more accessible to the children of middle-class families, or to those who cottoned on rapidly and adopted the mannerisms. The one who smiles self-deprecat-ingly and says, 'I hope you won't mind me bothering you, sir, but might I have my book back if it's convenient', wins approval and assistance. Less likely to make friends and succeed at school, is the one who shouts ''Ere! What about 'aving my book back, then!' All too often, reproval over mode of address, after what to the speaker may have seemed a perfectly reasonable request, leads to bewilderment ('What's he on about?') and resentment ('What's he got against me?') The teacher will have to learn to be buttonholed in a variety of manners. This will call for maturity, self-assurance, humour and a readiness to be firm but kindly in maintaining standards and style. ('Yes all right, you can have your book in a moment. Just let me finish what I'm doing.')

He has to retain the responsibility for care and guidance, while abandoning any desire to dominate. The teacher cannot abdicate from leadership to become a functionary or facilitator, but he might heed the useful words of the psychiatrist David Cooper:

Perhaps the most central characteristic of authentic leadership is the relinquishing of the impulse to dominate others. Domination here means controlling the behaviour of others where their behaviour represents for the leader projected aspects of his own experience. By domination of the other the leader produces for himself the illusion that his own internal organisation is more and more perfectly ordered.[1]

In my first years of teaching, I spent some of my most rewarding time on playground duties. At those times, boys and girls I knew from my classes, and others I did not know so well, would come and chat, leaning over a railing or walking round the field. They talked about everything under the sun, to me, to each other, sometimes intensively, sometimes swerving off on to other subjects, following whatever interested them, or telling those endless marvellous jokes that they think you have never heard. The bell for afternoon school would put a stop to all that and our formal roles would be resumed. Back inside, the barriers were upheld by students on their side as much as by us on our side. But my belief that what went on in class was the real thing, and those expressive exchanges on the playground were not, had been undermined from the start. (Playground duty as a subversive activity?)

The teacher who has come down off the daïs, moved among his class, listening and exchanging, is closer to his other self on the playground. If the classroom door is open so that the students may come and go in pursuit of their work, the teacher has a more complex job. He has to have the imagination to suggest tasks and a comprehensive knowledge of what resources are available. The classroom may itself house a range of equipment and materials, books, work-cards, pictures, maps and extras that may never have been supplied by the education authority, such as a second-hand typewriter or a jumble-sale slide viewer. Then the teacher needs to know the total resources of the school, formal, such as the library, film-strip collection, tape and videotape recorders, and informal, such as who has a cider-press or a stethoscope or a steam-engine.

Beyond that he has to know the resources of the neighbourhood, whether there are local archives to hand, where there are examples of different styles of architecture, a museum, a slaughterhouse, the dates on the gravestones, the bells in the church tower. Not every teacher in the school will know of all these resources, so between them they need to construct an index of local resources, objects and people. Within the school it should be possible for any teacher to supplement what he knows of the locality with this pooled information by access to a central bank of resource details.

At the same time, the teacher needs to become skilled socially so that he may have these local resources available to him and his students, not cut off from them. He needs to learn just how to get on with, or get round, the town archivist, the parish verger, the oldest resident, the canal lock-keeper and so on. He has to learn to negotiate with more adults than his predecessors, and perhaps consequently to be less pompous and bossy, to be less of a moralist and more of a neighbour.

If his concern is for his students' learning rather than for teaching his way through a syllabus, then the teacher of any subject will soon find himself at its boundaries and straying into others. His concern in an open school will not be to return the wanderer to his own safe fold, but to decide at what point his own limitations of guidance have been reached and a colleague with another specialism should be referred to. This can only be possible when each member of the staff knows the special expertise and interests of the others, for it is upon those that the curriculum hangs. An open school can never be simply a collection of specialists, however well organised. Every member of staff needs to have an understanding of its whole curriculum and a concern for the progress of his students through it. The school needs to advertise for and appoint staff accordingly. It is no use appointing a brilliant chemist only to discover later that he avowedly has no interest in what happens elsewhere in the school as long as he is inducting the young into the rigours, delights and mysteries of his own subject.

So the teacher has to be resourceful, technically skilful, expert in his own subject and knowledgeable about the rest of the curriculum. He also needs to be increasingly understanding about group interactions. The pursuit of enquiry by students directed to the whole diversity of resources, means that some will work alone, some in pairs and others in groups. The teacher must be sensitive to when he should engineer these formations and when to let well alone. This requires perception of the characteristics of each individual working with him, and certainly recognition that they are all different, never to be treated as if members of groups, however limited in number, were all the same.

Inevitably, study in small groups, awareness of the whole scope of the curriculum, centrality of the individual's learning, movement in and out of the open classroom, point towards co-ordinated work between teachers, not only within a subject department, but across the disciplines. It is the latter, interdisciplinary co-ordination that becomes increasingly necessary as study crosses those boundaries and the teachers need to keep track of it. This, in turn, imposes a new demand upon the teacher.

In the earlier days a British teacher could pride himself on his autonomy within his classroom. Provided that he got results and caused no disruption to his colleagues, he was free to develop his own style, which at times might be very eccentric. He might enter on a bicycle or deliver his discourse while lying out flat along a bookcase, but provided the class did its work and order prevailed, no questions were asked. More to the point, he could decide when to spout, when to test, when his class should write, when read, when enjoy a joke and so on. But co-ordination within a teaching team means that autonomy is sacrificed to group agreements over timing, materials, themes of study and teaching styles. A hardy eccentric can be anathema to a team.

This collaboration does not end with the arrangements for teaching and learning. Assessment has also to be by some co-ordinated means. Increasingly over the past decade, teachers in a school and across schools, have had to work out between themselves the appropriate examinations for their students. Mode III examining has been a mystery or a bogy for many parents and employers, but put simply, it is a means of examination whereby: (i) the school works to a syllabus that it has compiled itself, to the satisfaction of the external examining board; (ii) the school sets the examination papers, again submitted for approval by the board; (iii) the candidates' scripts are marked against an approved mark scheme by the teachers who set the exam; and (iv) this marking is then moderated by the board's external examiner. The final award of grades and issue of certificates is the function of the board.[2]

The challenge to the teacher as assessor extends further. In a lot of Mode III examining, work completed by the student during the course may be assessed and allocated up to anything from half to the whole of the marks. This may help the teacher in part to assess elements of a student's work other than his performance, particularly his powers of recall, at the time of examining. If the teacher's aims are, among others, to promote the ability to solve problems, to retrieve information from diverse sources, to hypothesise, to negotiate with others and to work with them collaboratively, new ways must be found of assessing the extent to which they are achieved.

The degree of care for the progress and development of those in their charge means for the teacher a capacity to transcend the division of outlooks that have come to be called 'academic' and 'pastoral'. They represent, in theological terms, the most unfortunate schism and heresy of recent educational history. Regrettably, they were introduced with the large comprehensive schools in the 1950s and 1960s. The size and newness of those schools made the danger of children being lost or bewildered patently obvious. Each child on arrival needed to feel that he or she belonged to a smaller, identifiable group than the school. The Public School pattern of 'houses', derived from the grammar schools, was adopted, though without the distinctive separate accommodation.[3] There rapidly developed a standard internal organisation of a dual framework: one set of senior staff formed a structure of departments of study, responsible for what was taught in the classrooms, while another parallel set formed a structure of houses, responsible for discipline, guidance and personal care. The rank and file teachers were therefore servants to two masters, their heads of departments, and their heads of houses. Quite apart from the increased sense of subordination this created in junior teachers, it had the retrograde effect of divorcing what should be indissolubly wedded in any teacher, the care for your students' personal growth and advancement in learning.

In an open school, these two sides of the teacher's function are reunited. Learning is seen not as an acquisition of items, like picking strawberries, but as the flowering of a whole personality. It calls for a totally different structure to the one developed conventionally now in large schools, but one which in various forms has been tried successfully and is available for schools to adopt.[4] It needs to be, in any of its variants, an arrangement whereby the teacher with main personal, tutorial, pastoral responsibility for any individual student also engages centrally in that student's studies.

All that I have outlined so far in this chapter adds up to a demand for the teacher to be more accessible, more resourceful, more competent as an organiser, more aware of his neighbourhood, more collaborative with his colleagues. This will diminish his autonomy and reduce his privacy. The demand will be intolerable if it merely leaves him overburdened within a pyramidal hierarchy, once again, albeit in new ways, carrying out someone else's master plan. He has the right to expect a vastly increased say in determining the conditions under which he will do all this. Fortunately, the open school, with its flattened hierarchy and its mutable structures will afford just such opportunities.

Equal shares in the decision-making creates unmistakable demands upon the teacher, as well as making other demands more tolerable. In any form of participation or power-sharing, the participant needs to be mature enough to carry the accompanying responsibilities, and to withstand or use the tensions that will be generated. Participatory or democratic government is not about getting your own way, but about compromise and consensus, the art of the possible. Initial experience of such a system, in school, and probably any other institution, may lead to frustration on two counts in particular.

First, a desire to have a voice in *every* decision will be

found impracticable, since there are too many decisions to be made, and too many people wanting to be given time to speak. This is the Ancient Greek stage of a participatory government: it probably has to be worked through to the point where it is seen that the real essence of democracy is accountability, and members are satisfied to leave most decisions to other people so long as they are elected, not appointed, open in their proceedings and accountable to the general membership.

Second, severe frustration occurs at first when people find they have not got what they individually wanted, that the vote has gone against them. A straight majority vote is likely to cause even more resentment, since it means that up to 49 per cent may be opposed to a measure that nevertheless has majority support. It can be just another form of win-or-lose battle and lead to internal politics and chicanery. Much more satisfactory is the approach which accepts but works upon conflicts, examining differences, offering alternatives, and by means of compromises reaches a working consensus. Consensus means commitment and the obligation that then can be felt by all involved to uphold a policy decision, not to capitulate in difficulty but to keep to the decision and make it work.

The result of consensus government is a huge increase in job-satisfaction for the teacher, a much greater readiness to make a success of what has been agreed on. But it calls for a readiness to listen to others, to forgo the desire to win and dominate, and a developed sense of how other people operate. Our education system, with its emphasis on individualism, competition and authoritarianism is not an ideal seedbed for this kind of teacher. In time, open schools will breed teachers for open schools.

The student

Using this term instead of 'pupil' or 'child' can sound portentous, especially if one is referring to eight-year-old Patsy. But I am not: I am referring to the post-primary age –

which starts admittedly with eleven-year-old Patsy – and more particularly that new range in full-time compulsory schooling from fourteen to sixteen, the ones who in my generation were out in paid employment. All that I am advocating in this book is also pointing towards a melting of the hard boundary between full-time compulsory schooling and lifelong education. To assist in that identity between the learner in secondary schooling and the voluntary learner who may study anywhere, whether in the back room at home, or in industrial retraining, the term 'student' is a useful token.

The term 'pupil' also reinforces the concept of schooling as an interaction between one who is unformed, malleable, of interest only in so far as he or she will *become* a person but is not yet more than a grub, pupating, and the master (or mistress) who knows all there is to know, who transmits it to the pupil while shaping, moulding, the future man or woman. At its purest, this concept of education created the relationship of master and disciple, where the master, or guru, *is* the model for the disciple's becoming. We derive the very term 'discipline' from this relationship, implying the controls that will hold the disciple bound to the master and his way, until the time of graduation from novice to master.

The approach to study that I have outlined in Chapters 4 and 5 calls for a totally different role for the teacher than that of master. It requires a reciprocity of interest between teacher and student, a blurring of boundary so that, to some degree at least, the teacher is also a student and the student a teacher. Both pursue knowledge, the teacher with greater experience and skill which he imparts to his student, but with no predetermined outcome. The teacher is above all person-centred, more concerned with the student as he or she *is*, than as something to be formed, someone *becoming*, of interest mainly for what they may turn into. We don't know what will become of our students or of our children; we don't even know what they will need to know: we can only assist them as they are. The relationship of master to disciple or pupil is therefore redundant, as is the discipline appropriate to it. What we need to create is the discipline appropriate to the relationship between teachers and students in an open school.

Since I have been misunderstood, often wilfully,[5] on this point, I should make clear that I regard discipline as necessary for effective learning, only it must be a form of discipline appropriate to the kind of learning, and to the relationship between the teacher, the learner and whatever is being learnt. Teaching has too consistently been concerned with pupils producing the right answers. The teacher has posed the problem and the pupil has to work out the answer, which the teacher already knows. (Many will have shared the disproportionate fascination that I felt as a boy for the teacher's edition of the textbook that had all the answers at the back.) Now if the teacher's task is to direct his pupils towards the right answers, his skill will be in commanding attention while he explains the method, and increasing motivation on the pupil's part by rewarding success and punishing wrong answers. This calls for a discipline of obedience and concentration on the word of the master. Whether applied in kindly or brutal fashion, this was a discipline of stick and carrot. It is not surprising that for many people, 'discipline' means simply 'punishment' and most often of all, corporal punishment.[6] Most significantly, it was a discipline of teacher domination: the good teacher controlled and directed his class – the poor teacher allowed them to follow their own direction. The assumption was that, left to their own direction, the sheep would go astray, possibly turn into bullocks. Usually, to be obliging, the uncontrolled *would* run riot and thus fulfil the prophecy.

There is no doubt that any altered discipline has to be learnt. Pupils will not adapt easily after conforming to a discipline of close rule. A transitional period, if one is needed, will be hard and stressful. Of course, it is not needed if an open, person-centred discipline has been experienced at home and in early school. But certainly the discipline appropriate to study in an open school does not come easily. It is one that requires of the teacher the kind of rationality, competence and imagination already called for. It is one that demands of the student, of any age, a readiness to identify an interest, to experience the satisfaction of completing a stint of work well, to admit to boredom or failure honestly and without fear.

It also calls for a readiness to share with others the interests, insights, successes and failures that former disciplines made into private concerns.

Above all, the open discipline is one which will induce the student, step by step, to accept responsibility for his or her own learning, behaviour and morality. The student needs, more than in former generations, to grow out of dependence upon 'a magic helper',[7] someone to relieve him of the responsibility of choice, and to become both stronger in self-identity and the same time more able to work collaboratively. There is no contradiction between learning to be both autonomous and collaborative.

In an open school the student, like the teacher, will be encouraged to take a greater part in determining the conditions of study. The way to learn to do things, as any good craft teacher will tell you, is not to go on studying or talking about them, but to do them. The way for students to learn about autonomy, collaboration and the discipline required, is to engage in activities requiring them. The job of school is to provide ample opportunity and encouragement for such activities, and to supply guidance and supports at times of failure. School is a place where failure should be a chance to learn, not a source of ignominy. So the student will not only be encouraged to devise strategies in study, to take charge increasingly of how to learn, but will be drawn into the corporate decision-making of the school.

There is no excuse in an open school for a student, or a teacher, to complain passively about the arrangements for their work. They should both be able to find access to the machinery for change. The student may start by exploiting the close contact with teachers and their readiness to listen to suggestions for local change, be it even so modest a change as altering the position of a desk. (In my school days we would only dream of rearranging any furniture as an act of defiance.)

That should be a step towards participation in any meetings empowered to recommend larger changes. The student will have an important voice, not only in domestic issues like the price of coffee but in issues of curriculum, such as whether Classics or Business Studies should be taught to A-Level.

In an open school the staff will accept that they cannot impose a measure upon the students without their general consent, while by the same token the students will accept the reverse, that they can't impose a measure on the staff. There must be mutual consent for things to work and part of the student's role will be to contribute to the consensus.

In an open school there is no reason why any meeting other than one discussing a delicate personal issue, should be open to teachers and closed to students. In my experience, the contributions to discussion by students have, with frightening consistency, been more brief, cogent and constructive than those made by teachers. I am also convinced that the same would hold true at governors' meetings once students are accorded their rightful place on the governing body. They are quite unlikely, chosen with care by their peers, to be as unaware of the conditions needed for study, to be as long-winded, platitudinous, irrelevant, pompous and indiscreet as a number of those who get on to governing bodies at present.

There is a powerful body of adults who argue that students should be kept in submission, neither seen too prominently nor heard at all. The task of teachers, in their view, is to contain school students (and indeed university students), tell them what they need to know and come down hard on them if they step out of line or fail to learn their lessons. The pity is that this produces the sort of violent and fruitless outbreaks so dear to the Press: marches, demonstrations, walk-outs, lock-ins and so on. The most recognisable model of rebellion for the young is the football mob. A Head remarked to me in March 1978 that when school students were showing their objection to teachers refusing to supervise dinners, the only way his kids knew how to take action was to go to the football pitch and chant slogans.

Students need to learn the art of democratic politics in school. We have at least reached the point where Her Majesty's Inspectorate has come out in favour of school students being introduced to education in politics rather than kept in ignorance until plunged into employment, or unemployment, ripe for exploitation. This of course, will not go down well with the paternalists on county councils who prefer to see education as a sedative that will produce a docile citizenry. But if they wish to avoid destructive confrontations, not only with school students but with those they will have become in a few short years, we all have to learn the techniques of negotiation and the recognition in the other, with whom we negotiate, of a full measure of human dignity.

Finally in this section, what reply is there in the open school to the student who asks, 'What about exams?' The answer seems simple. Inasmuch as they are needed in our society, study hard and pass them. Only remember, once school-leavers are into their first years of employment, over half the examinations taken at school will no longer have any currency value worth speaking of. In the open school, responsive to the demands of students and society, examinations will be given full attention. But students will be encouraged to see that life is not just for living in the future, that school is not just a preparation for later on, but something to be lived to the full at every moment. The examination system is often made out to be a strait-jacket for teacher and student. More often it is a feather cushion under their bottoms, protecting them from the challenge of imagination, imagination in how to get the best out of the examination system, how to keep it in its proper perspective, how to use all the time that can perfectly well be kept free from examination work.

There is also now a sizeable body of evidence to support the prime importance of language, and particularly talk, in learning.[8] For the student who wants to succeed not only in understanding the broader problems of living through the twentieth century, but also in the more immediate task of passing examinations, there is no substitute for the understanding that grows from free and informal conversation, with fellow students and teachers. The open school should buzz regularly with the exploratory talk of a learning community.

The head teacher[9]

Within normal terms of appointment, a Head has usually enjoyed powers that can be considered under six broad headings. There is some variation in the extent to which governing bodies have retained control in any of these areas, and there are worrying current tendencies which threaten to take back powers from governors to local councils, but whoever holds these six cards is running the school and where governors have trusted the Head whom they have appointed, these are the cards that he has been dealt.

First, the Head has traditionally defined the objectives and the values for his school. He has operated within the limits of what the governors and parents expect, but this is seldom a problem if they have chosen the Head they want. (In other words, the constraints will not need to be spelt out as the chosen Head will be presumed to have internalised them.) The Head has seldom needed to make his objectives and values explicit. In fact part of his power has lain in leaving them implicit, or expressed only in ritual, so that they have not been exposed to rational cross-examination and consequent modification. They can nevertheless be clearly understood and thus effectively govern the school. Wherever the objectives and values are explicit, the Head has still won as he has been the mouthpiece of the school in all public statement.

Second, the Head has determined curriculum – what is taught.

Third, distinguished but related, is control of the internal organisation, by which the Head has had power over access to the courses of learning within the general curriculum. He has decided who has opportunity to learn what, who can study Latin and who has extra woodwork. He has controlled the timetable. He has decided how the pupils are grouped, who teaches them and, within the statutory requirements, how long they stay at school.

Fourth, the Head has distributed the available money. Therein lay one of his greatest sources of power. He decided how capitation allowances from the local authority are used: he can starve one department to build up another. He has virtually controlled the distribution of special allowances to the staff, thus having authority over teachers' incomes outside their basic salaries. In some authorities this distribution of additional payments is made by the governors, but the Head's recommendations to them remain crucial. This particular power can become – almost invariably does become – the most resented of all, especially when his distribution of favours remains secret. Through it the Head can control staff by promises, threats and bargains. At the same time, he is laid open to promises, threats and bargaining from the lobbying of his staff. It becomes very difficult for a Head to be sure when a teacher is being completely honest and frank with him, not saying what he thinks the Head wants to hear, and it becomes difficult for the teacher behaving in that way to retain self-respect, which is the main reason for the usual isolation of the Head: staff find it easier not to speak to him too often.

Fifth, the Head has chosen his own staff. The extent to which the local authority qualifies this varies considerably, but the Head can usually make his pick. In contrast with employees in industry, he cannot dismiss staff. But my main point is that it is the Head who has decided for his teachers whom they have to work with. They like his choice or lump it. This was all very well when we only had to tolerate each other in the staffroom and could retreat to the idiosyncrasies of our classrooms, but increasingly now we have to plan and work in close conjunction with these colleagues and feel a growing right to share also in their selection.

Finally, less obvious, but significant, is the degree of power that a Head has exercised through control of the media of communication. Quite apart from being the spokesman through the external media, via statements to the Press, letters to parents and so on, the Head has been able to assert his authority internally by such means as: (i) control of paper and print for circulating notices; (ii) convening and chairing staff meetings; (iii) conducting assemblies; (iv) access to public address equipment; (v) installation and distribution of telephones; and (vi) preparation of policy statements and reports. All this amounts to a one-way system of regulative communication, with negligible means of feedback for assistant staff or students.

In an open school, the situation will be totally different. The Head will have shed power, not just to the point of careful consultation, but having agreed not to overrule the staff and, further still, to abide by and operate on their consensus. This does not mean being reduced to a mere administrator, who executes the general wishes: the Head shares in the decision-making, and if he or she has been wisely chosen the experience and judgement brought to bear will be considerable. In other words, the Head must carry authority, but cannot be authoritarian.

The Head, deputies and whatever administrative staff there may be, will act on policy decisions that will have been made by the collected body of staff and students. The machinery for reaching this consensus may take various forms, but once a school has established a body of basic policy on aims and practices, the need to appeal to any kind of general assembly is much reduced, perhaps to once a term. What will be more necessary is a structure of intermediate bodies that will make decisions in the light of those policies. By these means, the Head will have delegated all five major areas of power listed above, either to the general assembly or to elected sub-committees.

To take two examples – appointment and finance. Obviously, appointment is crucially important. If the school is hierarchical, each member is ultimately responsible to the Head. It is necessary to win and keep his approval and patronage. If relationships with colleagues break down, that is regrettable, but if the relationship up the line of hierarchy to the Head is preserved, not too much is lost. Thus, if the Head's appointed man is rejected by the rest of staff, the system will survive. In a highly collaborative organisation, where the lateral relationship is crucial, the system depends on corporate acceptance, even if the Head's relationship with the staff is not a good one in every case. It follows that the selection of additions to staff cannot be left to the Head, but must somehow reflect the needs of the whole staff. Two necessities emerge from this: first, candidates short-listed must have time, at least a day, to meet the whole staff, taste the flavour of the school, open themselves in conversation and he seen in contact with students. Second, an interviewing panel must represent both the subject area of the post advertised and, to ensure that concern for the whole curriculum is satisfied, other areas that are not directly connected. Means must be found, before selection takes place, for staff views to be fed to the interviewing panel. And then, if the staff have elected that selection panel, it can abide by their choice and recommendation.

With regard to finance, it is an advance on what happens in many schools if the Head will only publish the distribution of available money with a budget. But to be fully open, to lay aside this major source of power, the Head must delegate the budgetary decisions to the appointed committee of the general assembly. In this way, the incessant bargaining process that now goes on between staff and Head is transferred to a group who must be accountable to the general assembly. The individual who wins special financial favour with the Head is unlikely to cut much ice with a committee of his peers, and if he does, since the proceedings will be open, there will be quite sufficient pressure to see the balance restored.

These two examples also illustrate the different degrees of mutability in an open school's structures. An appointment committee is virtually *ad hoc*, dissolving when the specific task set is complete. A finance committee will have the specific task of drawing up an acceptable budget, but administering it, hearing appeals, dealing with contingencies, will be a long-term job, probably for a whole financial year. It will probably meet regularly and its task will be arduous. However, to be elected to it will be a sign of considerable trust, and the experience that it affords will be beyond comparison with anything known about school administration below the level of deputy head in a traditional organisation.

The Head, or a deputy, may well be asked to sit on both of these committees, by virtue of the responsibility still carried *vis-à-vis* the world outside the school. Until any maintaining authority is prepared to be open enough to find an alternative to appointing a Head on contract to each school, then the Head is the one who remains accountable to the governing body and the local education authority. The Head is the one who has to provide an answer to the awkward question by either the governors, parents, the Director of Education, the Press or politicians. The head on the block is the Head's.

Governors

The very term is unfortunate. It suggests either prison or the colonial tradition that could say, 'go out and govern New South Wales'. That kind of directive control is inappropriate in any school today, far more so in the school of the future. At best, the term may be taken as a metaphor drawn from engineering: a device for regulating the speed and rate of change, a moderating influence.

The complexity of a school today, the new issues faced and the pace of development mean that a governing body, meeting infrequently, with members mostly committed to full-time work of their own, cannot keep abreast of what happens in school. At most it can receive reports and offer advice to the Head. It cannot possibly control the school except by using its powers to bring it to a standstill. With luck and management, it may have a chairman whose relationship with the Head is strong enough to enable him to keep attuned to the whole corporate complex.

The Taylor Report[10] of 1977 moved opinion a little towards the idea of a governing body being principally in the control of the school's local community. The issue is politically fraught since the core of every governing body is at present composed of nominees of the local government. This is done so as to preserve a balance of political colour on each body, but with the result that too many governors are appointed for their political party allegiance, not because of any commitment to the school. They frequently feel obliged to flex their muscles and by definition know how to play the committee game to their own advantage and to the disadvantage of committee amateurs who may be much more deeply concerned for the school. Far too often, and indeed increasingly, governors have put party above pupils and exploited their position for local political advantage. By contrast, governors with a high investment in the school, parents, students and teachers, press harder for what they know the local authority should be doing for it, and they maintain a closer contact with the school and its functioning.

The Taylor recommendations deserved more support than

they were given, but they did not go far enough. The advisory function of a governing body should be carried out by a partnership of the users, parents, teachers and students. These are the people who will see to it that a school gets the resources it needs. They will not be required to grace platforms in floral hats or chains of office. They will not be the people who send their own children away to other schools, presumably because the one they are prepared to patronise as governors is good enough only for other people's children. They will be the people for whom the school is at the centre of their own community, who study there or work there, have their children or grandchildren there, live near it and have occasion to visit it.

At present there is usually a division into governing body, parents' association, school council, adult student association, staff committee and so on. A Machiavellian Head can play one off against another, while a Head seeking some sort of corporate management may find himself falling apart attending all their various meetings. What an open school needs is a co-ordinated advisory body representing a balance of all these parties, sub-committees, elected officers, and the professional staff providing continuity, communication and coherence.

Notes

1. D. Cooper, *Psychiatry and Anti-Psychiatry*, Tavistock Publications, 1967; Paladin edn, 1970, p. 109.
2. It is a common misconception that Mode III examining is a do-it-yourself job in which the school awards its own certificates.
3. There are exceptions, notably in Coventry, where 'house' centres were built into comprehensive schools.
4. The best exposition of such a scheme in practice is given in Michael Armstrong and Lesley King, 'Schools within Schools, the Countesthorpe "team" system', in *The Countesthorpe Experience*, ed. John Watts, Allen and Unwin, 1977, Ch. 4.
5. The *Leicester Mercury*, 4 Jan. 1977.
6. For a fuller development of the question of discipline see my article 'Tell me what to do and I'll do it', in *Discipline in Schools*, ed. B. Turner, Ward Lock Educational, 1975. I now regret giving my paper the title I did. It led the *Leicester Mercury* to say that on my salary I should know what to do without being told, which in fact reinforces

my argument for a discipline that induces autonomy. The quotation
is from a little didactic poem entitled 'Obedience':

> Tell me what to write,
> And I'll write it,
> Tell me what to do,
> And I'll do it.
> Tell me what to shoot,
> And I'll shoot it.

7. See Ch. 4, pages 59–60, and note.

8. Much of this evidence is drawn together in the Bullock Report,
*A Language for Life: Report of the Committee of Enquiry Appointed
by the Secretary of State for Education and Science* (HMSO, 1975).
But the crucial influence has been James Britton, whose book
Language and Learning (Penguin, 1971) serves as a useful introduction.

9. I have examined the place of the head teacher in an open school at
greater length in a paper, 'Sharing it out: the role of the Head in
participatory government', published in *The Role of the Head*, ed.
R. S. Peters (Routledge and Kegan Paul, 1976), and reprinted in
The Countesthorpe Experience ed. J. F. Watts (Allen and Unwin, 1977).

10. The Taylor Report: *A New Partnership for our Schools*, HMSO, 1970.

7 School, community and regenerative education

There is an old Hindu story about six blind men who discover an elephant. Each one catches hold of a different part of the elephant and each declares he has encountered something totally different from the others. The one who finds the trunk says he has caught a snake, the one who feels round a leg thinks it is a tree, the one with the ear says it is a windmill and so on. Community and community education are much like the elephant: we tend to define it according to the limb we have caught hold of.

The Tavistock Institution is said to have listed over 200 quite distinct current uses of the term 'community'. Without going into such refinement, I want to look briefly at five ways of looking at community education, each with a distinct form of organisation. This is not because ultimately organisation is the most important thing, but because each of these forms of organisation grows out of a particular concept of community education, and I want to clear the ground for presenting a notion of lifelong education that has itself certain implications for organisation.

The first way of defining community education is as a school that makes its facilities available to its neighbourhood. The argument for such practice is based partly in economics and partly in cultural demand. Since the days when a school house needed little equipment beyond blackboard, chalk, slates and crayons, the capital investment of plant has grown to the point where perhaps a quarter of a million pounds' worth of machinery, books and other resources has been installed in one school. This may well sit idle for most of the day in term time, and all day during week-ends and holidays. Especially since a lot of the equipment will become obsolete before it is worn out, the community, which has paid, indirectly, for this provision, should be able to share its use.

There is a whole catalogue of equipment, ranging from sewing-machines to trampolines in any secondary school today, that adults as well as full-time school students would like to use given the chance. And, it is argued, they have a right, as citizens, to use it.

Not only should equipment be available, but also space and tuition. Teaching has to be paid for, but space is *there*, and there is force in the argument that to spend public money on libraries, theatres, laboratories, workshops, and then lock them up for most of the time, empty, is a social folly.

When Henry Morris, as Secretary for Education in Cambridgeshire, was developing the idea of the village college in the 1920s and 1930s, he had a cultural ideal, backed by an economic argument.[1] He wanted to revitalise a moribund rural community, reliant on the towns and cities for entertainment, cut off by lack of cheap transport, shame-faced by its own traditions and lacking facilities to develop leisure crafts and study. Morris's hope of creating active, self-reliant communities was that shared by, and to some extent derived from, Leonard Elmhirst of Dartington, and Rabindranath Tagore.[2] Morris, in contrast to these two other men, saw his mission as one of bringing cultural enlightenment to the benighted. Elmhirst used business expertise to promote local forestry and rural industry, helping local people to make their enterprises economically viable. Morris, on the other hand, taking his leaf out of Plato's book, created premises where people would be surrounded by works of art.[3] He invented festival ceremonies, imported lecturers and artists, in an attempt to give, some would say impose, a culture.

A less paternalistic approach to community education was developed in Leicestershire from the late 1950s onwards by Stewart Mason, Director of Education and his successor Andrew Fairbairn. It was Fairbairn who coined the phrase 'open access', and it sums up the basis of the Leicestershire community colleges. At least in intention, these colleges have been secondary schools whose facilities have been made available to the public. In practice, since their principals have been the headmasters and headmistresses of the schools, the extent to which the public has been allowed the access has varied. The needs of the school student have always come first, and although the community colleges have been built with additional space in respect of adult and youth activity, pressure of school numbers has usually prevented any equally shared availability of the resources.

However, the extent to which public access has depended upon economics is shown in recent years when public expenditure has been cut back. In education community provision has tended to fall an early victim to any axing. The users of the community colleges have been forced to be more self-reliant. This is not an entirely unhealthy shift, but it has unfortunately discouraged the poorest, including the elderly, the handicapped and the young parent. It has also caused the college to guard closer to its bosom those items of equipment subject to wear and tear (potters' wheels, badminton nets, typewriters) which the county council can no longer maintain or replace as it formerly did. If 'open access' leads to a decline in the quality of the facilities of the school, then the schoolteachers will hoard them and the economic justification of 'open access' breaks down.

A second form of community school, a pedagogic one, is one where the teachers and students exploit the resources for learning within the locality. It may operate as a reciprocation to the first form, in which the public exploit the school, but it is quite possible to have either in the absence of the other. The starting-point for this particular form is the simple realisation that all the necessary resources for learning do not lie within the school.

There is a long tradition of 'outings' from school, quite apart from treats: the 'nature walk' must have a respectable history and museum visits have a time-honoured place in the calendar. The point at which a qualitative change has occurred is probably when such visits cease to be additions to the course and are seen as an essential requirement. It is at the same point that the learning from the external resource ceases to be a passive activity and becomes a positive interaction in which the student takes the initiative.

In many cases it is the outside agency that has taken this step forward before the school. Museums like the National

History Museum at South Kensington introduced enquiry schemes, providing suggestions and work materials, for schoolchildren during their holidays and probably many more were getting on in this way with work of their own than were doing so at the prompting of their schools.

The school functioning in any elaborated way of this sort within its community will promote a whole battery of student enquiries that will help to answer the questions that arise inside school. These will include examination of evidence in remains, the church, castle, town hall. It will increasingly need to monitor what is happening at the present time in urban development, road development and land development. There is increasing reason to believe that it is less important to retrace the movements of a medieval battle or the outline of a Roman wall, than to plot, as it occurs, the demolition of a town centre or the carving out of a ring-road through good agricultural land.

The neighbourhood of almost any school is rich with potential for study, historical, geographical, sociological, linguistic, aesthetic and scientific. Some of this may involve silent observation followed up by deductive work in school (for example, recording traffic density at different times of the day, to be analysed later as part of a town-planning exercise; or counting the lamp posts in sample streets in order to estimate the extent of local street lighting and the energy expended). Inevitably, such activity, away from school and the teacher, will involve students in personal interactions. They will need to learn, and be helped by their teacher to learn, how to conduct these interactions. They will need to develop the personal skills of negotiating, self-presentation, the interpretation of body-language, along with the sheer need to respect other people as they are.

Therefore, the justification for this practice of sending the student out to learn in the streets is not just that with discretion and a camera they will be informed by the objects around them, but that they will have to devise social strategies to get what they want. One of the powerful implications of Chapter 4 of this book is that people are experiencing an increased number of short personal contacts, in their work and their social lives, and in order to survive and prosper, they need to learn how to cope with them. Whether we welcome or deplore the fact, the techniques characteristic of the street arab (swift appreciation of situations, facility with exchanges of language, banter included, ready wit and an eye to the main chance) are increasingly more conducive to such survival and success than are those of the old country dweller (caution, silence, suspicion). These may be promoted in school by such means as simulation exercises, but the skills will remain hypothetical until employed for real purposes.

And the teachers will need to learn a lot in this direction. It is not enough to help the student devise a questionnaire and then turn him loose. There is a whole realm of learning about the ways of anticipating the response of others. This will be essential training if we are to avoid the sort of blunder that I once observed when two fifteen-year-old girls were indiscriminately handing question sheets for a study of marriage to visitors leaving the school gate. The sheet included the questions, 'Do you believe in sex before marriage?' and 'Do you approve of wife-swapping?', while the visitors included the vicar. There are ways and ways.

The earliest documentation of this kind of externalised curriculum that I know is provided by Crawford Somerset in his study *Littledene*.[4] A New Zealander, appointed headmaster to a small town school on the plain of Canterbury after the First World War, Somerset realised that the classroom lessons he was trained to give bore little relationship to the lives his children led in that farming community, and to the experience they already brought in with them. Using the contacts he was already making among farmers, craftsmen and townfolk, he built up a network of learning points at mills, farms and workshops, and took his pupils out to learn about measurement, computation and craftsmanship on the spot.

Crawford Somerset was already working within a colonial tradition of mutual help within the community, and yet that tradition has all too often produced a sharp distinction between 'book-learning', what they taught you in school, and real learning in the university of life. New Zealand has

not escaped the preoccupation of school with academic learning, the scholastic heresy that the essential truths could be
taught to all pupils within the confines of the master's cell.
Even so, the other tradition, championed by Somerset, has
flourished and there are enterprises such as Four Avenues,
mentioned in Chapter 3, and other organisations for community education that have taken one final logical step.

This step brings us into a third kind of community education – one that has no institutional premises other than an
office. Four Avenues may depend upon programmes of study
deployed about the community in Christchurch, but it has a
home base. One unforeseen discovery in its early months was
the extent to which its students used and seemed to need the
domestic base, with its familiarity and security. My own
conviction is that for most learners, but particularly the
adolescent, a diverse and roving programme of study requires
the support of a safe base and a personal tutor to provide
unity and stability. Given that, there seems no reason why
particular study should not then take place wherever the
resources are available.

The fully decentralised community education scheme seems
likely either to be part-time, or built around co-ordinated
but stable learning points. In Nelson and Masterton, New
Zealanders have created just such schemes. In each case, a
group of local people has analysed local needs, won political
support and appointed a director. He has essentially been
provided with an office, a secretary, a phone and a car. The
brief, then, was to identify groups with learning needs, to
find the teachers and other resources necessary for meeting
those needs and to tie them together.

While in New Zealand, incidentally, I had it brought home
to me very plainly that the *pakeha*, the European, is too
individualistic and competitive to have much notion of community in its true sense. I was told this openly by the Principal
of a community High School. 'But we are learning now,' he
said, 'by going to the Maori and the Polynesian. They have
always known.'

Behind the arguments for an organisation without walls,
stands the whole case for de-schooling, made familiar by the

passionate advocacy of Ivan Illich.[5] There is no need to summarise his thesis, nor that of Paolo Friere.[6] Both are important, available in print and deservedly influential, but the strength of their cases derives from the deplorable state of education for the depressed majorities in Latin America. Their exposure of organised schooling as a means of suppression and indoctrination cannot possibly be ignored, in the advanced Western nations as well as any banana republics, but the solution of abolishing schools is of little practical help in Europe where institutions are workable but in need of radical reform. The British certainly are averse to tipping out the baby with the bath water.

There are two more ways of defining community education that I wish to raise, and both relate to control. The first is an American model, in which we see the aims, curriculum, ethos and staffing of a school determined by a school board. The board is chosen by local election and may, therefore, be represented as democratic. The defect is that it is also intensely political, with little certainty that those elected to the school board will represent any cross-section of local interests or attitudes. Those who win places and keep them, like those on any local council, will be those skilled in political manoeuvring, expert in committee procedure and public presentation. Their sensitivity to educational needs and the operation of schools may not go beyond the catch-phrases and slogans that win elections.

The fifth model is that of the community school controlled by its users – parents, students and teachers. It is a perfectly practical proposition to put a school into the hands of the users, so defined. A governing body could represent the interests of those who had commitment to the school's prosperity. However, it could work most effectively if self-supporting, and therefore as a working model, likely to be realised only in the most wealthy localities, and consequently likely to obtain for itself resources that would be denied to others, in other words prospering at the expense of the less wealthy. It would be to prevent this happening that any local education authority would require representation on the board of governors of any of its schools. Only in this way could local government protect the interests of its wider community by a fair distribution of its resources.

The Taylor Report, as mentioned already,[7] has advocated a balance of control by representation on governing bodies of teachers, parents, local authority and (where possible) students. At the time of writing this, each party, except the students, is angrily voicing suspicion of the likelihood of being dominated by the others. There is no reason, however, why it should not work. The really important thing is that with a true balance, no one sector can dictate to the school. It may turn out to be another case of our having to learn from our children. Certainly from our children rather than from Goethe, for whom man was either the hammer or the anvil. The need for the open school and open society to teach us how to collaborate is urgent. The lead is certainly not there in the council chamber, nor on the floor of the House of Commons.

None of these five models adequately depicts the possibilities for community of the open school, which by definition will promote an interpenetration of school and neighbourhood. What it offers is a composite model, resembling in certain features each of the others. It would make its resources available to the public throughout its working hours, it would infiltrate the neighbourhood to find its resources and tap them, it would arrange its ethos and curriculum to be responsive to its users and neighbours, it would have balanced powers of government between teachers, students, parents and other accountable bodies in the immediate locality, and it would facilitate learning and leisure activities within its neighbourhood but outside its own walls.

In such a relationship with its neighbourhood, the school would have an enhanced likelihood of meeting some of the needs discussed in earlier chapters. Take first the need of the student in full-time schooling to appreciate that learning is not confined to what he is instructed to do, or what he finds out inside school. By going out into the community he learns to pinpoint problems and devise strategies for solving them. For instance, he wants to find out for a study of local public transport, what the destination is of each of ten people waiting at a bus-stop. When he sets out, he thinks that is the problem. Then he discovers that the immediate problem is not that at all: it is how to elicit that information from ten people. How does one ask them? Why should they tell him? How can he explain his purpose to them? What will he reply if one of them says it's a pity they don't give him something better to do at school? The teacher who knows what he is doing will be as interested to find out later how these secondary problems were solved, or not solved, quite as much as what answers have been given to the destinations problem.

In such an exercise as this hypothetical one the student will be learning not only about personal interaction but about the skills of negotiating for information. He will need to be preparing for those brief, thin relationships that will feature later in work and out. He will also be seeing the essential extension of how learning occurs through interactions inside school to the ways of finding out in the outside world. It won't all be conducted at bus-stops: it may be in an office or a factory or a shop that the contacts need to be made.

Then consider the consequences of school being open to those whose compulsory education is over, whether two or three years ago, or twenty or thirty years ago. Where space permits (as it has been planned to in counties like Cambridgeshire and Leicestershire) there should be little problem in providing for adult day classes. These will at once exert an influence on the school, though it may be minimal if the space provided is carefully segregated as in the early village colleges and community colleges. But even if the 'adult wing' is carefully placed well away from classrooms, some interaction is inevitable if only because school students may encounter adults in a corridor visiting the office.

When I opened Les Quennevais School in Jersey in 1965, the point of contact in daily routines between school and community was the library. This had a door at one end into school and one at the other into the car park. The civilising effect upon the young was unmistakable, and the adult borrowers soon had a much improved understanding of the students' own work and interests. The key was a branch librarian who was not only serving the public library, but deeply interested in the life and work of the school. It is an interesting footnote to add here that when I worked at Sawston Village College (1953–58), the shared library, far from being a fruitful mingling place for young and adult, was a constant source of conflict and division, for the simple reason that there was a school staff librarian and a county branch librarian neither of whom had overall control and responsibility.

If I could have rebuilt Les Quennevais, I would have placed the library in the centre and not in a wing. I later argued[8] that a community school needed a good central attraction where all ages would mingle in doing something they enjoyed, like roller-skating. I was delighted to learn soon afterwards that Henry Swain, Nottinghamshire's county architect was putting the same idea into practice, but with ice-rinks. The Sutton Centre at Sutton-in-Ashfield, is a town comprehensive school with a recreation centre and ice-rink in its middle.

The benefit of Les Quennevais's library and the Sutton Centre's ice-rink has been that a shared interest in the use of the place could be experienced by adult and adolescent. Not just an observed interest, but one that was *experienced*. There was no need to point a moral or labour the point to the participants: it came to be felt. If we go one step further and open up the more orthodox school facilities, the workshops, laboratories and the classrooms, not to observers but users, not in separate classes, but mingling with the full-time students, an even greater transformation begins.

For a start, the school student will ask the adult student – 'Why have you come back here?' The almost inevitable answer is – 'Because I realised that I didn't learn all I wanted to when I was at school.' The implication is obvious, though the adult will sometimes spell it out – 'Your education doesn't finish when you leave school.' (Some will say it only started at that point.)

The next observable factor for the school student is that the adult student is highly motivated and will work hard and keep deadlines, even though carrying commitments outside, at home or in employment. To use a good old-fashioned term, they are an example. The wise teacher will not point this out: he will simply let it take effect.

This is not all that follows in the wake of this Jericho effect. With the walls down, the inner rituals and manners of school can no longer continue in the isolation that preserves them. Not only will the young ask questions about aims and methods, but teachers will ask them of themselves and modify their behaviour too. Kids are less likely to use obscene language with adults in their class, but by the same token teachers are less likely to shout and intimidate, or preach and pontificate. I once heard a sixteen-year-old ask a thirty-year-old woman in her class – 'What would you have felt like coming back if we had all been in strict uniform?' The reply was – 'I wouldn't have come back.' Some braver souls would have, but many others would not. In other words, a silent pressure would push the school into becoming more like the outside world, less uniform, less regimented.

But I want to look further at what happens when an adult returns to school. The first step of deciding to come back is by far the largest. Over and over again in listening to those who have done it, I hear them refer to the fear and anxiety they had to overcome and above all their battle with a resurrected sense of failure. They associated school primarily with failure, in a deeply personal way. They had not just failed exams or to come high in class, but in some global way to have failed as persons. I often feel that our academic, competitive, exam-ridden school system, in spite of those who have made the grade, was most consistently successful at producing failures. How frequently I have heard parents say, 'I was no good at school', and know they have passed on to their children that sense of school as the judgement seat to which all are called and most are found wanting.

This sense of inadequacy could last a lifetime. Here is a woman in her thirties remembering that

> . . . to fail the eleven-plus was to fail totally. Most of the professional jobs became impossible to contemplate, but a more disastrous effect only became apparent in later life, the

inability to think on one's feet, a talent which is absolutely essential if one is to survive the 'Human Jungle' and be considered a success. In short we were sold out and destined to become also-rans, little cogs, never among the winners.[9]

What an indictment – the 'also-rans'. We used to say that since the eleven-plus failures were not fit for academic training they were intellectually disabled. So we gave them increased time in practical subjects, cookery, woodwork, 'rural' science: always apparently *concrete* operations. Above all, what we did was to deny them the opportunity of handling abstractions. And handling abstractions means power.

And so a second, even more powerful, disincentive for the would-be returner has emerged. The nature of the betrayal, what it is that they were supposed to have failed at, cannot easily be identified or communicated to anyone else, because of its own very nature. To express it is an exercise in abstraction, and that is what they were conditioned to believe that they could not do. All my teaching life I have wept inwardly for those countless people who have resignedly said – 'I'm not very bright: I'm thick.' All right, suppose a few *are*, the majority of those who have come to accept this are *not*, and I've wanted to cry out to them – 'It's a lie. You are not. Every boy and girl has within them the potential of a blazing intellect, a creative imagination, and success in some direction.' But by denying the chance, we have convinced them of the contrary.

For the returner, something must have stirred them to think that perhaps the system lied, that they were not as hopeless as they thought. It may have been some opening at work, or a loving spouse, or, once the door was opened slightly, a glimpse of what all those children of the unlettered failures were doing nowadays at school. Hope was regenerated, but confidence would be low.

The first approach to the community school for the returner is likely to be for a standard, easily identified course. 'I wasn't allowed to take O-Level English at school and I'd like to have a try.' There might early on be a vocational element in the return: this, too, will tend to be conventional – 'I've brought my own children up so I'd like to qualify for nursing.' Behind these immediate suggestions will usually lie a great deal more potential that has never been sorted out, for the reasons stated above. For a start there is that unanswered question – 'Am I any good at anything half-ways intelligent?' With this may go a long-felt desire to grapple with those forbidden and tantalising abstractions, such concepts as Energy, Power, Structure, Beauty, Society, Growth or Communication. The returner may enter with one stated purpose, but with growing self-knowledge and guidance may convert it to another and leave finally with a purpose that would have been beyond conception before arrival. It may take years, though not as many as may have elapsed since failing the eleven-plus.

The implications for the community school are mainly two-fold. Entry for the returner must be made inviting rather than threatening, and staff need to be trained and skilled in the guidance that will be necessary. I have already outlined that formula for promoting learning – Security plus Competence plus Challenge.[10] It can equally be applied to the adult returner with whom the teacher is regenerating a power to learn. Given that the returner has already experienced challenge by coming back at all, the community teacher has to provide security and competence.

The likelihood is that the usual trappings of school, the Head's office, the seat in the corridor, will reawaken earlier trauma. Reassurance needs to be given in the form of homely settings, such as a cup of tea and somewhere for small children to play. There should be something on the wall less formidable than the framed hockey team. There is no reason why such a provision should be entirely separate and special. The real implication is that the entire school should look more like a club and less like a barracks.

Then once the returners realise that they are not alien to the school, they may be ready to talk to staff about what they might do. There is no reason for this to be hurried. The initial entrance may be made without any firm intent of study, but for, say, a morning for mothers to chat. Alternatively, members of all-adult groups might be welcomed into the use of day school social facilities, like break-time coffee, and begin to talk in that context. But most schools would have to change if their break-time coffee arrangements are to be shared between teachers and students, adult and adolescent. But then, many bastions crumbled at Jericho.

Only in this way can returners, faltering over that long sense of failure, unused to the abstractions, begin to articulate their own needs and ambitions. As it does happen, though, they need skilled, professional advice on the openings and opportunities. Teachers, by and large, already need to learn a lot, and keep learning, about careers guidance for their secondary school students. To this must now be added, if not for all, then for those with specific community tutorial responsibility, a comprehensive familiarity with outside agencies, courses in Higher and Further Education open to adults and contacts with individuals with relevant experience that they are willing to share. There are implications for teacher training that I shall return to in Chapter 8.

There are considerable difficulties arising from school becoming open to its neighbourhood, and much imagination needs to be put into surmounting them. By way of summary and conclusion, I shall list just seven of the opportunities afforded by such a development, note certain barriers likely to be found in the way, and suggest some strategies for overcoming them.

1. Opportunity to reformulate long-term curriculum aims in the light of community expectation. This may give rise to a re-examination of old questions such as – 'What is school for? What is learning?' But there are two major barriers. The first is the generally conservative public notion of what a school is, still too likely to depict it as a place to contain children and tell them all they need to know. The second is the conservatism of the teachers themselves as a body, and the concept of the teacher as someone there to master the pupils and instil them with knowledge and manners. The strategy that may overcome both is by hook or by crook to get the public in. It may be the Head's strategy to change attitudes on either side, it may be the teachers' or it may

be the public's. If only a two-way traffic can be started and maintained, changes will commence on both sides of the wall, until it collapses.

2. Opportunity to exploit the neighbourhood for its resources for learning. Two barriers come to mind. One is the resistance that the neighbourhood may put up to finding the young neither in employment nor confined safely to desks in class, but prowling around counting lamp posts and interrogating bus passengers. The other is the unreadiness of teachers to engage in the necessary mingling, consulting, negotiating, indexing, so as to find, use and remember these community uses. A strategy for the first barrier is to *serve* the neighbourhood as well as use it. This must go a long way beyond redecorating old ladies' kitchens (while certainly not excluding it). For instance, the local council might welcome a research programme into local needs and services (which might even entail counting lamp posts). The answer to the second problem must surely lie in teacher education, initial and in-service, responding to the need for these additional social skills.

3. Opportunity for the school to open its resources to the community. There are practical and financial barriers here. Fully open access can and does lead to premises being in use for twelve to fifteen hours a day. Most of these uses produce mess, from wood shavings to chalk dust, and there are problems of organising cleaning and maintenance, since there is less chance of this being carried out during use as it is, say, in a hotel. This is further complicated by multiple use of areas, where for example a lunch-hour recreation room may need to be made ready for afternoon mothers' session where babies will crawl around. This calls for advanced industrial cleaning techniques and one strategy may be to charge this to the users where the local authority cannot provide it. The financial barrier, referred to earlier in the chapter, applies equally to maintenance and repair of equipment, and here, too, the necessary strategy may be one of finding an equitable mechanism, controlled or monitored by the users, for raising and disbursing funds to cover the costs.

4. Opportunity to demonstrate the practice of lifelong

education to those still in compulsory schooling. This will be afforded not only by returners who mingle in school classes but also by the old and the infants who may use the facilities. The biggest single barrier is the equating of education with examination. The existence of any major school-leaving certificate then reinforces the belief that finishing school means finishing with education. On the other hand, the teachers may employ the strategy of using the community contacts, in school and out, to draw up examples of learning continuing from the cradle to the grave.

5. Opportunity to replace the tradition of teacher domination, aided by ritual controls, with a new contract by consent and collaboration. The barrier to this will be erected in part by teachers whose attitudes were formed in a different ethos, in part by those with a political interest in subjecting the broad mass of the young, not their own children, to coercive control. An effective strategy here is to organise the voice of (*a*) the parents who realise their children are getting a better educational deal than they did themselves, and (*b*) those who were failed by the system and are now experiencing their regenerative education. If the school cannot win the support of its parents and students, it is doomed: if it can win that support and have it voiced, then the old guard and the noise-makers can be ignored. No politician with any acumen is going openly to oppose that support.

6. Opportunity to enable adults, through a secure and welcome setting, plus professional guidance, to identify and articulate their needs and their aspirations. A very real barrier is raised by the limit reasonably placed by the teacher on the extension of his role. Counselling and social work require special aptitudes and training. A teacher may find this well beyond what attracted him to teaching and a distortion of a role already being adequately filled. Getting round this one is difficult. Training is only of value where the student-teacher has some vocation. One thing is sure, that where a maintaining authority has acted upon the conviction of need for community education, it must provide additional staff, qualified for the work, to any existing establishment. These staff in turn then

need all the support possible in spreading and sharing their skills and insights.

7. Opportunity to disprove the belief that adult and youth have a natural mutual antipathy, to prove that they can work and play together harmoniously, reach decisions and act on them in trust together. The main barrier will be that of prejudice on both sides, and the answering strategy will be the devising of joint activities that depend for success upon community support from all age groups. There remains the honest concern over the need of adolescents to get away from adults, and the worry that community involvement may destroy the last refuge of the teenager from the surveillance and interference of his or her elders. Well, surely, they need the chance to be alone with their peers *some* of their time. We all do. And we all need the opportunity for occasional solitude. But not all the time. For far too long schools have shared the monastic tradition of enclosure from normal life. We can respect anyone's, or any group's need for periodic isolation without regressing to seven or more hours of it a day.

Notes

1. H. Ree, *Educator Extraordinary: The Life and Achievement of Henry Morris*, Longman, 1973.
2. L. K. Elmhirst, *Rabindranath Tagore: pioneer in education. Essays and exchanges between Rabindranath Tagore and L. K. Elmhirst*, 2nd edition, John Murray, 1961.
3. This became an increasing preoccupation for Morris. Shortly before his retirement in 1954, he invited R. A. Butler to open Bassingbourn Village College. Morris took R.A.B. on a tour and included the toilets. Pointing out proudly that each door was painted a different colour, he said, 'We like to think that even going to the lavatory will be an aesthetic adventure.'
4. C. Somerset, *Littledene: Patterns of Change*, NZ Department of Education.
5. I. D. Illich, *Deschooling Society*, Calder and Boyars, 1971.
6. P. Friere, *Pedagogy of the Oppressed*, New York, Seabury Press, 1970; Penguin, 1972.
7. The Taylor Report, *A New Partnership for our Schools*, HMSO, 1977.
8. John Watts, 'From Ally Pally to Ally Poly', *The Times Educational Supplement*, 22 Oct. 1971.

9. Hazel Oxley, 'Seen and not heard: a comment on learning through discussion.' in *The Countesthorpe Experience*, ed. John Watts, Allen and Unwin, 1977.
10. Chapter 5, p. 78.

8 Some implications for teacher education

When I taught at the London Institute of Education I used to ask my graduate students why they wanted to become teachers. Almost invariably they answered that they had a love of their subject that they wished to convey to others. This was no doubt affected by their having first taken a degree and then continued to post-graduate certification in teaching. College of Education students preparing for the B.Ed. will have had an intention to teach initially and their study of subjects will have been coterminous. I suspect even so that their starting-point will usually have been a desire to impart something to children.

If what I have argued so far is valid, that the emphasis must pass from what the teacher wants to teach to what the learner wants to learn, then a desire to convey some body of knowledge, or a love of subject, must be converted into a more open desire to promote learning, a love of study, of making and doing, but with a precise content that in the end cannot be defined in advance. This is in no way to deny the need for every teacher to have studied one or more subjects until conversant with it in depth. To repeat an earlier caveat in a different form – basic skills and data in such essentials as literacy and numeracy must be learnt by the teacher and conveyed to the children. But these basics are the tools, and the ends will be shaped as time goes on by the students themselves, rough hew them how we may.

In the short space of this chapter, I am not attempting to examine in any detail the existing structure or content of existing courses of teacher education. Ranging from the initial steps in a B.Ed., through in-service diplomas, to advanced degrees involving research, the field is wide and complex. I shall therefore limit myself to certain points that I find to have implications for the design of such courses and suggest some ways in which they might be implemented. I shall be satisfied if they open up the debate already taking place about teacher education. Any modified forms that may result from that debate are for others to determine, fashioning them to the other demands and exigencies.

However, to start at the beginning, recruitment might call for rather different qualities than in the past. In doing so, a contribution will have been made to modifying the aims and measures of success in the sixth forms of the schools. Recruitment to teaching has traditionally drawn upon those who have succeeded within the school system, and are therefore most likely to perpetuate it. They have usually been the ones whose teachers wanted their pupils to become like them; they have usually been the ones who wanted to become like their teachers, to be a reincarnation. Miss Jean Brodie could re-create Miss Jean Brodie, not with her brighter, most perceptive and adventurous spirits, who rebelled and broke loose, but with the ones who remained fixated upon her.

Teaching needs to attract the enterprising, the innovator, the challenger, instead of the conformist and the regressive. When I taught graduate students, I was regularly dismayed by the way some of the most promising teachers decided to turn to some other occupation after their first spell of school practice. It was never the classroom and the classes that put them off: it was always the pettiness and confinement that they discovered among the staff. Whereas their contemporaries engaged in industry as graduate trainees were given opportunity to prove themselves or be out on their ear, those in teaching got the message to keep a low profile, toe the line and carry on with security of tenure and an eventual pension. The more enterprising either traded that security for the chance to make their mark elsewhere, or went into teaching knowing that there were going to be battles. The conformists who had worked the system to get where they were by conforming would find their place in school by continuing to conform.

That is not to say that schools want or need the disruption of raging reformers arriving as probationers with the banners of change streaming behind them. The beginner will have to learn a lot and with great role-humility. But, with decent self-restraint, he should be afforded opportunity in school from the start to share the insights gained from a fresh eye, a keen mind and an eagerness to get on. The probationer teacher, after all, should be at an intellectual peak, recently graduated, and the school staff should be ready to pick his brains, not snub him, overburden him with work, or reduce him to tea-orderly like some fifteen-year-old apprentice.

Recruitment has to compete with business and industry so as to avoid that awful drift into teaching by those sixth-formers who can't think of anything else to do. Colleges, universities and polytechnics need to send out their scouts, as do Shell and ICI, to fire the bolder spirits who would welcome the challenge, excitement and danger of school-teaching. We need those with enquiring minds, a shown capacity to solve problems, imagination, sociability, humour and a toughness of body and psyche. We don't need the respectable meek, who are waiting to be told what to do.[1]

Having recruited a promising entry to education courses, what might we hope they will learn before stepping back into school as young teachers? Chapter 6 suggested new roles for the teacher, and I wish to run over their implications for teacher education. Precisely how these demands are to be met will vary from course to course, college to college. I shall incidentally, use the term 'college' in general reference to university departments or faculties, institutes and colleges of education, polytechnic schools of education or wherever teachers are in preparation.

There was a time when too many colleges had the reputation of being converted manor houses where the staff emphasised gracious living, epitomised by cut-glass on the high table. This may well have given a sense of security to some, and of challenge to others, especially if they had been more accustomed to tea in the kitchen. But it seems rather remote from the general run of schools and the exigencies of a post-industrial, pluralist society. Security plus competence plus challenge is as good a recipe for college as for school, but different forms might be more appropriate today.

Within the life of the college, security needs two sources.

One is the individual care and guidance that should be afforded by staff who are more preoccupied by teaching than by their research. The other source is assured conditions for thought and study. Just as within school, these provisions should go without saying. And yet they don't. One of the most common complaints I hear from university students is that they have far too little access to their teachers. Since those teachers, unlike their counterparts in schools, do not spend all their time lecturing or holding seminars, it is a fair question to ask what they are doing that is more urgent than being available to their students. Similarly, a student might expect as of right to have access to the resources of learning and a place for study in peace and quiet. This is far from being always the case.

The college teacher and the supervisor of students in school practice share responsibility for developing competence, in study, in preparation, in organising successful learning in school. Practice periods in school will provide sufficient challenge and threat when the time comes for them. It is important that the college does not allow the shock to be sudden and rude. In other words, the period prior to school practice must go beyond the provision of security and competence to providing its own challenges and shocks. There needs to be a course that is far more dramatic than one of lectures and seminars. Built into it, there should be occasions that require the exercise of practices such as those outlined in the following paragraphs. Then the students will have begun to prepare for playing the role of teacher by doing, as well as by thinking.

For a start, preparation for collaborative planning and execution of programmes in school could begin with students being confronted with problems that will only, or most swiftly, be solved co-operatively. The armed forces long ago pioneered the posing of such group problems, and there is much to be said for college students attempting similar physical tests. There is an obvious analogy for teachers in the task of using a limited supply of ropes, planks and crates to get all the members of a group over a six-foot fence without touching it. Cross-country orienteering with minimum resources is another group challenge, and there are innumerable others. It is not difficult to make the transition from such physical challenges to group problem-solving indoors, where curriculum and lesson strategies are thrashed out.

The college staff should be competent in monitoring and advising on group interaction. They should be resourceful in suggesting exercises, games and follow-up study.[2] They should not be too concerned with their academic dignity, but be prepared to share in their students' exercises. There certainly is an extremely limited place on staff for the guru whose students will sit at his feet.

In valuing these interactions, the college teacher should have a clear understanding of the indispensable role of language in learning. By arousing a corresponding awareness in the students, the taboo on talk in schools will receive another overdue nail in its coffin. Reference has been made already to the importance of talk in school.[3] Students should be encouraged to study basic texts, such as Vygotsky's *Thought and Language*,[4] and evidences of the fruits of such theory in, for instance, the published findings of Douglas Barnes,[5] whose work has done so much to relate theory to classroom observation.

The essential lesson is not that discussion enhances learning, like a dob of cream on the top, but that it habitually facilitates learning that would not otherwise have taken place. John Dewey said that, 'Knowledge cannot be the idle view of an unconcerned spectator.'[6] Knowledge is the sense we make out of experience, and man's principal means of accomplishing this feat, what essentially distinguishes him from all other animals, including the higher apes, is the use of language.[7] There is now ample evidence to show that talk in groups is crucial to this learning and problem-solving, not in stately debate, not in sticking too precisely to the point, but in the fragmented exchange of statement, speculation, anecdote, joke, irrelevant or irreverent stray thought – in short, less of a discourse and more of a chat.

Of course, if the talk, conversation, chatting, is to get anywhere, its original problem needs focus. But what is also necessary, and for many students has to be learnt, is the capacity to listen. There is a distinct danger that students who at school succeeded in the role of passive listener, will not have learnt to listen except to their teachers. As teachers themselves they may all too easily assume the role of those they listened to at school and lecture the next generation in their turn. Listening to one's peers is a necessary transitional step towards listening to one's own students. A group of student peers will provide the most effective corrective to any one of its members who starts to lecture them.

A group that has come to respect individual differences among its members will be in a position to learn about teacher-group functions in school by going into action in college, not just in simulation, but in tackling real problems. The group that has hoisted its members over that six-foot fence, and has talked through its various prejudices, can take on a task such as planning and resourcing a project, either in college studies, or as a programme in school practice. They will learn about the division of responsibilities, about pooling ideas (or 'brain-storming'), chairing and reporting. They could, if their college is realistic, learn about budgeting and assessment of the constraints that limit and modify any ambitious plans. All this will be learnt by doing, rather than by hearing lectures on it.

In Chapter 6, reasons were given for the need for teachers increasingly to become collaborative, resourceful and also skilled in their interactions with the community. The college then must become less monastic than it used to be: teachers for the open school are most likely to graduate from open colleges. Just as in school, so in college we are unlikely to find most of the resources for learning catalogued away in the library and media-centre. Of course, the student must master the techniques of retrieval from, and the replenishment of, those resource banks. But he must also discover the ways of sorting out what can be learnt extra-murally by local exploration. It is incumbent upon the college, therefore, to set tasks that involve combing the surrounding town and country for their learning possibilities, and contacting members of the local community so as to give and take, help and learn. Only in this way will the college be preparing the students for playing a full part in a community school, unless such schools are to continue in dependence upon the specific community work of specially designated community-tutors. What I have argued for ought not to result in minority options in college for community work, nor for a small group of students who will maintain a supply of community-tutors in school, but for an essential element of community involvement that is shot through the college experience of all students.

The 'mature student' has long had a place on college courses, though regrettably often in a segregated group as if youth and crabbed age would not mix. If the young teacher is to be aware of education as either a lifelong or a regenerative process, there is no better place to develop that awareness than in college. Although very few schools have yet opened their classrooms to the adult student (in the way that many Leicestershire schools have done), most colleges have done so for some years. As long back as 1965, 14 per cent of students entering college, were aged between twenty and twenty-five, while a similar percentage were over twenty-five.[8] While a lot of mature students, who answered the call to return to teaching in the early 1960s when there was a shortage, enrolled at day colleges near their homes, it does not affect my point that most young college students have opportunity of contact and exchange with the mature entrants.

Far from organising separate courses and facilities for their mature entrants, colleges should capitalise on their presence. The eighteen- to twenty-year-old students, many still with reservations about teaching as a career, and usually with much to learn about taking responsibility for organising their own lives and learning, stand to gain considerable insights from these experienced adults. Most of them have had to make hard decisions and have often made sacrifices to embark upon their studies.

Not untypical was the Brixton vicar's wife with four children who was one of my graduate students at the London Institute. She would arrive at my seminars like me, a few minutes early, having already got her children off to school, the meals for the day prepared, her shopping done, and her homework in order for the session. We would chat about measles and school meals as the rest of the group drifted in, breathless, telling us about the terrible problems of sorting out the morning and the London transport system. She leant over backwards, as she put it to me, 'to avoid being auntie to them all', probably more successfully than I leant over backwards to avoid being headmaster to them. Over the course of the year though, not one of us, and I include myself, had failed to benefit by learning something from what she brought to our group.

The parallel with late returners in the schoolroom, mentioned in Chapter 7, should be clear. The very presence of such a one, who has opted and made the effort to get into school, poses the question of why learning may be desirable. The students who have had the experience of working with mature entrants while at college are the more likely to value the introduction of mature students into their classes when they have started teaching at school.

Of course, one category of mature student in college is the experienced teacher. Those teachers undergoing 'in-service training' as it is called, may be following part-time courses without interruption of their own teaching, or they may be on secondment from school for a full-time course. Either way round, they present a rather different case to the mature entrant to initial training, those who have not yet taught. The problem for the college is how to draw on the considerable experience such a group will bring between them, without swamping and daunting the novices. There is strong argument for keeping such experienced students, whether following courses for a diploma, for a M.Ed., M.Phil., M.A. or Ph.D., together in their studies. The college staff tutoring them must have the humility and good sense to use the skills and the insights that such a group will have brought with them. These will range from organising skills, to case-studies of individual children and detailed knowledge of the internal operations of schools.

If the changes necessary in school are to occur with practical wisdom and care, but at less than a snail's pace, then the greatest hope lies in the agency of experienced teachers who have had the opportunity to study, reflect and modify their position and their attitude. At present, far too little importance is attached by governments or local education authorities to the funding of long-term secondment of teachers for advanced study. More faith seems to be accorded to short conferences and courses of one or two days' duration. These hardly scratch the surface, do little to change attitudes and a lot more to consolidate them.

All attempts to challenge and modify a teacher's position, especially in the company of his local colleagues, poses a threat. In the face of that threat, the natural reaction is to justify one's present position. I am frequently invited to speak to in-service conferences organised by local education authorities, and can distinguish at once between an audience that has assembled for the first time (and possibly last time) and one that has had even a day to exchange a few blows, relax and then drop defensive postures. The fresh audience does not really listen, except to extract anything that will support a stance already adopted: their questions frequently indicate this attitude, or, even further, betray a desire to have heard things that were not said at all, in order to agree with them or attack them. A group whose members have got to know each other react in a totally different way. They have already defined their positions, they are ready to come out from behind the defence works, knowing where the fire will come from and how to treat it. The input of a visiting speaker can then be examined with less at risk, and may actually be listened to.

If the teacher on active service needs a day or two in supportive surroundings to trust coming out from his slit trench, then short in-service courses of a week will serve some purpose, but not much. At the first trumpet call, the teacher will jump back over the parapet to the safety of his prepared position. That is why in-service courses spread out over even a year on the basis of one or two evenings a week are ineffectual. They may enable new skills to be learnt by those motivated to learn them – for instance how to use reprographic equipment, how to make a film strip or how to assess examination scripts. But they will never make possible a major shift of role on the teacher's part: there is far too much at stake when he returns to school next day, or next week or even next term.

In my three years on the staff of the London Institute coming straight from a period of headship, I was able at first to share the experience of teachers on secondment for one-year courses, and then to reflect upon that experience. Any teacher, but particularly any senior teacher, carries with him or her a heavily stamped role. It has seldom been entirely of one's own choosing: other people, one's colleagues, one's students, their parents, their neighbours, all have strong expectations of how a teacher will think and behave in a whole range of situations. The role-set is ascribed to one as much as adopted consciously. After a while one may harbour existential doubts about who you are inside that suit of closely articulated armour. To change suit, or even replace it piecemeal, is almost impossible unless ample time is provided.

In the course of a year, and only in that time, a detached reappraisal of the habitual role becomes possible. In terms of an academic year, it is the period up to Christmas that is agonising, being prised out of the shell and left naked and defenceless. This sense of being cruelly dispossessed may result from study, the discipline of a good tutor cracking the joints of one's prejudices under the weight of a major text – Piaget, Vigotsky or Chomsky; it may result from some revelation of redundant role. I experienced the latter towards the end of that first term out of headship one day when I went to my room and found that some maintenance man, without let or hindrance or apparent regret on anyone's part, had put my desk, up-ended with my scooped-up papers dumped on top, on the landing outside. My shrine was desecrated. What is more, as I went about telling people, nobody was in the least bit sympathetic. On that day, five months after leaving my headship, and only then, was my self-image as headmaster shattered. It was very salutary, not least because until then I really believed it had already been abandoned. It has never been resumed.

The assembling of a new role, sometimes a new persona, by the teacher on a long-term secondment, comes with, and like, the new birth of spring. The changed teacher will have learnt both to generate sound theory from experience and to underpin future practice with sound theory. It is my belief that no educational expenditure will be better justified than funding teachers of ten years' average experience to follow full-time courses for a year on secondment. The James Report on teacher education recommended one term of sabbatical leave in every seven years. This was known to be inadequate, but thought to be realistic. It amounts to one year off in twenty-one years' teaching, and although this sounds pitiful it is still more than most teachers achieve.

In summary, the progress towards more openness in schools will be achieved at a pace determined principally by the school-teachers. No amount of exhortation or coercion by outside agencies will have lasting effect except with the willingness and competence of the teachers inside. Teacher education, initial and in-service, holds the key. The keyhole is the situation in school where an accumulation of circumstances, sometimes fortuitous as much as planned, makes a leap forward possible. The example that I can best attest to of this happening is analysed in Chapter 9.

The teacher who will be in training and watchful for such circumstances of change will have undergone a preparation that takes account of the foregoing. That teacher will be disposed to face new situations, work collaboratively, be inventive and resourceful, be concerned with the whole curriculum, be skilled in social interaction within both school and neighbourhood, be aware of education as a lifelong process and ready to work with diverse ages and groups. Above all, that teacher will have learnt the supreme importance of awareness of the other person, of listening with outer and inner ear, and of respect for that other person, particularly his student, whose autonomy is to be honoured and whose work is to be interrupted only with the utmost caution.

Notes

1. A much fuller study, though now in need of up-dating is contained in: W. Taylor, *Society and the Education of Teachers*, Faber, 1969.

2. The most useful single text that I have found in this respect is L. Abercrombie, *The Anatomy of Judgement*, Penguin, 1969.

3. The role of language in learning. See Ch. 6.

4. L. S. Vygotsky, *Thought and Language*, Cambridge, Mass., MIT Press, 1962.

5. D. Barnes, et al., *Language, the Learner and the School*, Penguin, 1971; D. Barnes, *From Communication to Curriculum*, Penguin, 1976.

6. J. Dewey, *Democracy and Education*, Macmillan, 1916, p. 154.

7. For development of the idea of language in the 'role of spectator' and language in the 'role of participant', see:
   (a) J. Britton, *Language and Learning*, Allen Lane, Penguin Press, 1971.
   (b) J. Britton, et al., *The Development of Writing Abilities 11–18*, Macmillan (for the Schools Council), 1970.
   (c) N. Martin, P. D'Arcy, B. Newton and R. Parker, *Writing and Learning across the Curriculum*, Ward Lock Educational, 1976.

8. The James Report, *Teacher Education and Training*, HMSO, 1972.

9 The lessons of Countesthorpe in the 1970s

Countesthorpe College opened in 1970 as a comprehensive community college under the Leicestershire Education Authority. It was innovative on a scale unprecedented for a maintained upper secondary school. It ran into early difficulties and opposition, but survived intact to remain throughout the 1970s as the closest approximation yet to an open school. Much, though not all, of its early difficulties arose from the challenge it offered to conventional schooling, and much, though not all, of the initial hostility it aroused stemmed from its being so unlike what a school is still generally supposed to be like. It weathered the storms and won acceptance from its users without sacrifice of aims, making a breakthrough that has attracted attention all round the world. It should therefore be possible to study its achievements and shortcomings with an eye to lessons for the open school in practice.

Countesthorpe has been written about by many hands,[1] but too much of what has been published concentrates on the spectacular and controversial opening years. It is more significant to consider the developed functioning of the college from 1973 onwards, when it had become what it was intended to be, with fourteen- to eighteen-year-olds in full-time schooling and an established relationship with the neighbourhood and its adult users. Since descriptions of this can be read elsewhere, I shall summarise the peculiar features of Countesthorpe in operation, and then proceed to the lessons that it seems to me it may provide.

For a brief account of Countesthorpe, I shall describe five aspects:

1. Architecture.
2. Government.
3. Relationships.

4. Curriculum organisation.
5. Community involvement.

This does not represent an order of importance: the features are interdependent. The sequence is merely convenient for exposition.

1. Architecture[2]

If you happen to fly over Countesthorpe College (and aircraft do use it as a landmark), or if you examine its plans, you would find that the remarkable physical characteristic is its circularity. It has been likened to a pineapple slice, with its serrated outer edge and the clean hole in its middle. If, however, you visit it in the normal way and tour it, what will strike you first is that it is all on one level, and secondly, that it is divided into diverse and irregular-shaped spaces. Occasionally, you find a classroom of reasonably orthodox shape, but it is certainly not the norm. There are instead large areas that can be sub-divided by furniture, and clusters that combine open spaces, classrooms, smaller office-like rooms and storerooms, in easily self-contained units. Communication routes are formed by a web of passages that either radiate from the central courtyard to the periphery, or curve gently around that centre intersecting the radial routes. The effect is at first disorientating, especially when you find that as you continue your tour you end up where you started. But then those who use the college don't spend much time touring it, and what they notice is that it is quick and easy to move from any one point of the building to any other. For a school designed to house 1,400 students, it does not feel oppressively large, and no part of it seems remote.

The architects, Farmer and Dark, were briefed to provide for ease of movement and flexibility of space. They were also directed, for the first time in Leicestershire's development of community colleges, to integrate the additional provision for adult and youth activities with the main body, instead of designing separate extensions for those purposes. This design reflected a definite stage of thinking about the nature of upper secondary schooling and community involvement on the part of Stewart Mason, the county's Director of Education, and Andrew Fairbairn, his deputy and successor. The building thus has certain symbolic qualities which I for one have found to increase in strength over the years, and which represent an extraordinary general vision on the part of the designers. Prominent among the features that I would call symbolic are the following.

Being circular, the building has no front or back, no façade and no rear exit. There are many entrances; one of them admittedly is a main entrance because it is nearest the main gate, but all of them are heavily used. One result is that nothing is hidden, all is equally accessible.

Then, although areas have specific designated uses, they lead one into the other and boundaries are blurred. Only music has a detached block used for one specific purpose. Even extended as it is from the areas of drama, and physical communications, it is isolated, in my view unfortunately. Otherwise, designated areas flow one into the other. For example, if you make your way round the workshops on the western periphery, you will pass through machine-shops, into the vehicle-maintenance area, and thence through Control Technology, a meeting-place of engineering theory and practice, finding eventually that its further door has led you into the science complex alongside the physics laboratory.

Similarly, although one area was originally labelled in the designs for Community and Youth, nothing confines it to those uses. The main space available for social mixing combines kitchen, dining area (that makes a good dance floor), coffee bar and fixed units of tables and benches around the sides that are regularly used for study during working hours. Here staff and students mingle before school, at breaks, after school, or in the evenings to relax and chat. Alongside it in one direction are 'team' study areas, while on the other side is a large room, originally empty and now fitted around with seats, alcoves, cupboards and a servery for refreshments. In this space in the course of a day may be seen a succession of infant play-crèche, lunch-time clubroom (for socialising or for games like table-tennis, billiards and darts), welfare clinics, youth club, film-shows and so on. Thus, it serves as a meeting place, a social focus, but without being separate. Boundaries are blurred, with the suggestion that there is no hard and fast distinction between school and community, work and play, young and old, inside and outside.

The most distinctive aspects of curriculum organisation as they have developed at Countesthorpe, which I shall describe a little further on, could not possibly have been foreseen by the architects. What they did was to help considerably in making such developments possible by leaving enough non-specific space and allowing just enough flexibility. Similar developments could occur in a more conventional building: there is no justification for saying that nothing of Countesthorpe's achievement can be repeated without similar buildings. Nevertheless, the design of Farmer and Dark has been conducive, both materially and spiritually, to the developments and their informing ideas. Almost any rectangular module of design creates vertical and horizontal sequences that suggest hierarchy and order of merit. Certain values will be embodied in the construction, and to some degree those who regularly use the building will either absorb those values or consciously rebel against them.[3] Countesthorpe is no exception. Whether the architects intended it or not, the building is in harmony with a participatory, non-competitive social structure that promotes diverse personal interactions and mobility.

I suspect that it was for what it thus symbolised that the college's architecture was attacked and ridiculed locally, rather than for the flimsy fittings and leaky roof that were so much more easily singled out for criticism. There were defects in detail, to be sure. The notion of an open library, for instance, seems to me to have been a mistaken application of the concept of openness. Openness does not mean *uncontrolled*, as long as we live in this world, otherwise we would need no locks on any of the doors (an early lesson that some of the original Countesthorpe staff had to learn). So the library, with its seven different exits could not safeguard its books. However, significantly, the layout made modification possible, so that by 1974 there was only one door to the library and it was able to assume its central function, as near as possible to the centre of the building.

A permanent shortcoming is the enclosure of too many spaces with top-lighting and no eye-level outlook. Considerable relief would have resulted from a few well-placed small courtyard gardens to puncture the main body of the building. But these are minor flaws in what I have come increasingly, after seven years of daily use, to regard as a school design of genius paralleled only by Walter Gropius in his creation of Impington Village College.

2. Government

Countesthorpe has a board of governors whose articles of government are identical to those of all the Leicestershire community colleges. Also the Principal has a contract from the local authority that bestows the same powers and responsibilities as would be expected elsewhere. The community users have a council with exactly similar articles of management to their counterparts around the county. But there the similarities end. In other respects, the internal government of Countesthorpe is unique. The powers and authority traditionally vested in the Principal have been delegated and shared in such a way that the determination of policy (following that crucial initial policy decision of the Principal) and the final appeal internally is to the collective body, the Moot. The Moot consists of all the staff, teaching and non-teaching, and all students and parents who wish to participate. It is a pragmatic arrangement in that the Moot has no legal validity and could not possibly work if everyone exercised their right to participate. It is effectual because it does not need to meet more than once or twice a term and because it seldom attracts more than a dozen students or one or two parents. In the early months of 1970–71, the Moot met frequently until it had thrashed out a body of policy and procedure. As this has remained virtually unaltered, it is worth recording here as it was drawn up at the end of that first and undoubtedly dramatic year.

Government – a statement of constitution as at August 1972

(i) Subject only to the laws of the land and the regulations of the education authority*, the Moot has, in relation to the school, absolute power to make decisions on policy and to control executive action.

(ii) The Principal remains personally responsible to the Governors and Education Committee for all decisions by the Moot and its committees and for all executive actions. He has delegated the right to make such decisions and to control such actions to the 'whole body' of the school instead of to individual heads of departments as he would in a normal school. In the case of the present incumbent he has agreed not to use a veto on any decision or action, but reserves the right to resign if a decision of importance is taken, which offends his conscience.

(iii) The 'Moot' for the time being shall consists of all professional staff, part-time or full-time, of the school, the full-time staff of the Community College and all ancillary staff.

(iv) That Upper School students – defined as 4th year and above – shall have the right to attend and to vote.

(v) The Moot shall set up four committees each consisting of a quarter of the staff, each to sit for one term. This Standing Committee shall elect both its own Chairman and Secretary, and the Chairman for the Moot. It shall meet weekly after school, to decide: (*a*) agenda for any Moot; (*b*) present matters of policy; (*c*) interpretation of policy; (*d*) minor decisions that lie uneasily between executive action and policy. It shall carry out preliminary discussions on Moot agenda and ensure that a backing paper to items on the Moot agenda is produced.

(vi) That the full Moot shall only meet to discuss important matters of policy or challenges to the decisions of its committees. At such meeting, no decisions shall be taken after 6 p.m.

(vii) The Moot shall delegate either to an individual or a committee the task of drawing up the lists for the four

---

*including, obviously, the Articles of Government

committees.

(viii) The Moot delegates to 'department' committees, consisting of all staff, professional and ancillary, as voting members and any Upper School students who can attend, talk, vote, the right to make policy decisions affecting the work in their own area, *provided* these are within the policy laid down by the Moot. Decisions *must* be taken democratically.

(ix) The Moot delegates similar powers under the same conditions to teams and any other sub-committees set up by Standing Committee.

(x) The Moot delegates to the individual members of the staff their appropriate executive power to carry out its policy or the policy of the committees. Such executive actions are open to challenge in the Moot but only on the grounds that they violate a policy decision.

(xi) Meetings can be called at will to discuss actions (e.g. distribution of capitation), but such meetings will not take decisions. Their purpose is to gather or to give out information.

(xii) No decisions have been taken on what is a quorum or committee.

(xiii) No decisions have been taken on the size of majority to pass a motion: practice has been to postpone for further discussion any close decisions if they are of major importance or if any members feel strongly.

The whole Moot, which has at times involved up to 100 people, is obviously too unwieldy for detailed business. Its agenda is always limited to a single issue of some weight. The multiplicity of intermediate decisions, neither fundamental nor minute-by-minute, are handled by other bodies, committees and individuals who are accountable finally to the Moot. Foremost among these is a standing committee of staff and students which holds office now for one-third of the year, consisting at any one time of one-third of the staff (thus giving everyone a term of duty) and a representation of students. Their meetings are open to everyone; anyone may place an item on the agenda and speak in debate; only the committee may vote. Each standing committee elects its own chairman, vice-chairman, and secretary. The agenda is published in advance and its minutes afterwards. The standing committee meets weekly,[4] and is expected to work through its agenda. In this way nobody, staff or student, need wait longer than a week to have an item raised at committee. The committee may decide on an issue, refer it to a sub-committee or working party, or direct somebody to take action. A major issue may cause a Moot if they feel the issue is weighty enough, or if they challenge the decision of the committee.

The chairman of the standing committee does a lot more than chair the meetings. He or she prepares for meetings by collecting information and follows them up by checking that action has been taken. This involves a lot of contacts over the week, and regular interaction with the Principal and deputies, commonly referred to as the Executive. The in-service management training for chairmen is extensive.

Sub-committees may be *adhoc* or permanent. In either case, membership is by election and held for no more than a year before re-election. An example of *ad-hoc* operation is the formation of an appointment committee to fill a vacancy. As is normal practice, appointment is the prerogative of the Governors. At Countesthorpe they interview for Principal and deputies, but delegate to the Principal and staff the means of selection and recommendation of all other staff appointments, sending a representative only to Head of Department interviews. The standing committee, or the Moot, will decide on the nature of the appointment and choose a panel which has balanced representation of the subject area in question and the rest of the staff. One of the Executive joins the panel, and for a senior appointment, so will one of the governors. The appointing committee will word the advertisements, which always follow the following pattern: 'Wanted, a teacher concerned with the whole curriculum of those he teaches and qualified to teach x or y.' Short-listed candidates are asked to spend a whole day at the college, and before they are interviewed, the Appointing Committee, in an intensive tea-time session, takes comments from anyone concerned. They are in no way mandated: the committee takes heed of comments and questions, interviews and decides on its recommendation to the governors. No one can ever blame a poor choice on anyone else: everyone is committed to making a success of each newly appointed member. Where, rarely, there is a failure, everyone shares responsibility for any remedy.

After appointment is recommended, such a committee disbands. An example of a long-term committee is that elected to govern finance. Control of disposable moneys is usually the principal instrument of a head teacher's power. There is no way of knowing at present how many head teachers disclose to their staffs precisely how much money the school has to spend or how it is divided up, but it can be very few who have other than a secret budget. Even where the Head publishes the internal budget, so that every department knows how much everybody else has been allocated, a sizeable sum for contingencies may remain at the Head's discretion. It then becomes a subject for bargaining between the Head and the assistants in the same way, if on a more limited scale, as is the whole capitation figure when no budget is issued. At Countesthorpe, the Finance Committee, having heard all bids, pleas and threats, issues its budget in fine detail. It also keeps check upon expenditure and with the help of the administrative staff, issues statements once or twice each term to let everyone know how accounts stand. Such a committee is very carefully elected, works very hard and has never been called on to resign.

I have elsewhere said that this may seem to reduce the Principal to the status of lift-attendant in a bungalow, but that is deceptive.[5] The altered role for the Principal in a participatory school government is a delicate balance between meeting the wishes of the internal users, and those of the external society and its agents, notably the parents, governors and local education authority. The tightrope would be an impossible one to walk without trust and confidence having been won from both sides. (Even then it can feel as if there were several hundredweight hanging from either end of your balancing pole, and Niagara beneath.) The role involves sensitising those on each side of the boundary to the needs, doubts, prejudices and limits of all those on the other. It should carry the authority of specialised information, usually derived from sources that do not share the same degree of openness; it should ensure continuity and co-ordination. Otherwise, in day-to-day operations, the Principal is dealing with situations and decisions very similar to those confronting any Head. The difference is that every decision and action will be guided by agreed policy and will be accountable internally as well as externally. And that is quite sharpening for the mind.

3. Relationships

For a start the relationships between staff, including the Principal and deputies, becomes markedly altered in a flattened hierarchy. Any respect shown mutually will derive from function rather than from status. As in *any* teaching situation a teacher will ultimately be respected only if he or she teaches well, strengths balanced against weaknesses. Where everybody is accountable to everybody else, there is a common bond and a common challenge, both within the smaller working groups and the body as a whole. Exchanges are frank, open, and possibly by a lot of common-room standards may sometimes seem rude or unprofessional. In fact, they are of the kind that any adult might make to any other, outside of situations bounded by rank and the threat of office. 'Where the hell then were you at duty time this morning?' might be said by any one member of staff to any other, regardless of salary scale or position, if it was thought warranted.

However, even more significant is the relationship between teachers and students. There are certain agreed rules that apply to everyone equally. These rules relate to conduct, respect for individual and corporate needs, governing such things as care for property, the conditions for uninterrupted work and sheer mutual convenience. But they apply alike to teachers and students, can be appealed against to the Moot or altered by it. The life of the college is therefore not rule-centred but rational. It is clearly understood at Moot and in committee that neither staff nor students can enforce a decision against the wishes of the other party. Thus rules may be seen *rationally* to coerce an individual, whether to stop a hypothetical boy kicking in a door or a hypothetical teacher smoking in a corridor, but the teachers do not exert any collective coercion. It follows clearly that it is unthinkable that the teachers should require students to wear any particular kind of dress as a measure of control. Similarly, disciplinary action is never merely punitive and physical force never threatened. In cases of transgression the order of the day is restitution, not retribution. If someone wilfully damages property, they are required, with the involvement of their parents, to pay the cost of restoration. Minor infringements are dealt with within the sub-groups rather than being passed on to a senior disciplinary officer. The ultimate sanction, open to appeal, is exclusion from normal work and group membership. Total exclusion is rare, and of course only effective since the desire to be included is greater than any enjoyment of exclusion.

Freed in this way from any sense of constant coercion, the students rub shoulders very openly with their teachers. Staff do not use a common room but share social facilities with students. They are thus constantly available, with no formal barriers erected. Direct use of first names is normal though not enforced. A teacher wins respect from the students only if a good teacher, as any good teacher knows. An indifferent teacher who sought approval by being chummy would only be despised. A teacher who knows his business, works hard and puts the real, learning needs of the students first, will, as in any school, not need any formal trappings to gain and hold that respect.

Countesthorpe consequently enjoys a remarkable absence of violence, vandalism or threat of either. It is commented upon almost invariably by visitors, accustomed in most secondary schools to at least some degree of threat between teachers and students. Teachers may feel the strains of work and constant exposure, but these are more than compensated for by the lack of stress caused by constant hostilities, hassle and confrontation.

4. Curriculum organisation

Amiable relationships in school could remain simply as mutual and unproductive indulgence which would soon pall into boredom and unrest. The purpose of all that informality is to facilitate the interactions necessary in a highly diversified arrangement for individualised studies. The basic organisation of the curriculum at Countesthorpe is neither one of streams, with groups of like ability, nor of mixed-ability classes. The emphasis is upon individual study and small groupings that form and reform in a very fluid way.

A more detailed account of the way in which this happens is given in *The Countesthorpe Experience*,[6] but may be summarised here. On arrival at the age of fourteen, students form 'teams' of about 100 to 150 in number, largely governed by friendship groups and the advice of staff at the feeder schools, but as far as possible so that each team reflects in smaller scale the range of intake across the whole school. Each team has its own clearly contained base in the school, with amenities for study, lockers, toilets and pegs. It is a mini-school within the school. A team is sub-divided into tutorial groups, and the tutors, five or six of them, offer a set of specialisms that will include between them, English, Maths and Social Studies. Those teachers work and plan as a unit, keeping the same student membership for the two years fourteen to sixteen. After two years the students either leave school or join the sixth form, and the staff receive a fresh intake.

Teams operate for a long session extending over half of each day. The tutors organise work, establishing between them a rhythm of activities engaging at different times individuals, small groups, class-sized groups (20–30) or the whole team. (Each team has in its cluster of spaces one in which all its members can assemble.) There is consequently a wide range of kinds of work that may go on in a team, with choices to be made by each student in negotiation with first their personal tutor and then others among the remaining four or five. The personal tutor is also responsible for con-constructing with each student in the tutorial group a personal curriculum and timetable covering both team-time and the other half of each day out and about in the other departments. The more adventurous student's timetable will eat into team-time, while some will add to team-time. Only rarely and by chance will two students end up with identical programmes. The permutation of subject combinations is limited ultimately by the master timetable, not by the class or stream or course that the student is in.

Therefore the team provides each student with Stability, Challenge and Contract. Stability is afforded by membership of a small unit, not just a nominal 'house' or a group that meets daily only for registration and notices, but one that forms the central arrangement for work and for spare time. Students arrive in team before school, may stay there at breaks and lunch hour: there is always at least one of the team tutors on duty. If a breakdown of any sort occurs during the day, students return to the team. They drop-in rather than drop-out. A student may arrange to change tutor within the team, and this happens from time to time after negotiations, often thereby resolving a personal conflict before it becomes critical. Technically, a student may apply to transfer to another team, following friendship changes, but it is a comment on the strength of the team's social cohesion that this rarely happens. 'Floaters' form fewer than 1 per cent of any age group.

This stability and close contact with tutors make possible the challenge of a wide range of curriculum options. The teams came into existence in fact, in 1972, to meet the problem of instability. The school suffered initial turbulence that resulted more than anything else from student confusion in the face of more choice than they could handle. Under guidance and from the secure base of the team, each student handles more diversity than was originally thought possible. Each team is a microcosm of its age group. Students are not pitted in competition against each other, except in competitive games. With individualised work, they compete each with his or her own potential under the personal assessment and encouragement of the tutors. Thus, no one succeeds at anyone else's expense. (No one competes unless there is a fair chance of winning, as any sportsman knows. In school, as elsewhere, constant losers become disturbed and resentful, while constant winners are resented.) In the Countesthorpe team, no one is stigmatised as a 'swot' or a 'dimmy': all are accepted for what they are, and yet this is without loss of personal challenge.

The personal timetable is essentially a contract. It cannot be altered or departed from unilaterally, but it is open to renegotiation. That renegotiation may lead to an alteration of times and need only involve the student, the tutor and the teachers involved: it may lead to a change of subjects and will then involve the parents as well. If it can't be arranged, all can see why: if it can be arranged, and it is agreed to be to the student's advantage, then it is. The basic membership of team and tutor group remains unaltered so that readjustment and attendant anxiety is minimal. The ability to negotiate does not come naturally: it has to be learnt. Like all other skills, it is learnt through doing. Usually in school, the youngster's inadequacy in negotiation gives rise to the teacher's impatience and justifies to him his pre-empting all the decisions. This leaves the student unskilled, or even, since he is unlikely not to have developed *some* skill of negotiation and autonomy outside school (if only to get himself there), de-skilled. Rendering a person de-skilled is probably worse than leaving him unskilled; it is retrogressive and belittling.

Of the many benefits accruing from this system of individualised timetable, it is worth selecting one, if only because it meets a frequently asked question – What about examinations? Countesthorpe has been able to maintain a higher *per capita* success for the sixteen-year-old rate than the local or national average, calculated across the whole comprehensive intake. One reason for this is that by avoiding streams and courses that usually mean decisions about groupings *before* arrival at fourth year (fourteen years), decisions about examination entry can be delayed as long as possible. For instance, by choosing very similar Mode III English syllabuses in both O-Level GCE and CSE the decision as to which of the two a student should enter, need not be made until Christmas of the examination year. Premature decisions which fix a ceiling on any individual's performance lower that individual's sights. Performance then fails to rise as it might have done, which naturally fulfils the prophecy and conceals the iniquity. (Pray it doesn't happen to *your* child.) By refusing to label anyone 'non-GCE O-level material' on arrival at Countesthorpe, we have regularly been able to encourage half our intake to take and pass English.

Perhaps I can conclude this section with a quotation from an account of herself by a sixteen-year-old girl, whom I shall call Judith, on the point of finishing her fifth year.

As you can probably imagine, the change to such a completely different school was very hard to get used to [after] rows and rows of tables and chairs, also lessons that everybody listened to. Everybody was educated with the same knowledge. Before I started Countesthorpe, my dad went to have a look round eight private schools in the area as we had heard so many bad things about it...

I think, looking back at it all now, I came with the attitude that I wouldn't like it.

After being at the school for six months I just started to be getting used to it. I fell in with a lot of friends and got used to all the teachers.

Oh, how I've changed my attitude now. I hope to stay on for my sixth form hoping to get a few more 'O' levels for my career, nursing, which if it hadn't been for this school I would never thought of.

What other school could you visit a hospital like I've done over the last two years and at the end of it been offered a job as a N.A. – Nursing Auxiliary, that's if I want it.

Well, let's put it this way [before I came here] I was told I wouldn't be capable of doing any exams yet I'm now taking seven CSE's and two 'O' levels.

I've got on really well especially in my fifth year not only on actual school work but making a lot of new friends. It's such a great atmosphere in this school and for anyone who intends to work there, there's no fault in it at all.

It's the right school for me anyway!

Reading between the lines of this refreshing essay one or two points emerge. The first is that it reveals some of the intensive local prejudice that has remained since the hostilities and newspaper campaigning of the early years. Judith's dad visited eight schools! It can be happily reported on the evidence of County Hall that since then the situation has been reversed and many more parents are opting in from outside the catchment area than are opting out to other schools.

Secondly, Judith's main adjustment was to a system of individualised study from a concept of learning in which 'everybody was educated with the same knowledge'. Her induction to a style by which students were expected to take increasing responsibility for their own learning was eased by finding others succeeding and enjoying school. Imagine the problem in the early years before any pattern was established to demonstrate to the novices what the initiates could achieve.

I think Judith might have found other schools that would have arranged her hospital visits. I am not sure how far elsewhere they would have arisen from the very core of her studies as this would have done. The team, in collaboration with the college's specialist community staff, arrange such placings and relate it to course work in team.

Certainly ceilings were raised for Judith, though it took her six months at her own estimate to look up and realise it. The last point is that at the time of writing that, Judith did not feel in any way that her education was going to stop yet. The sixth form is seen by her to be open for her needs.

5. Community involvement

There are so many doors by which one may enter and leave and re-enter Countesthorpe, that it is impossible to cover the point of community involvement adequately. Under the normal provision made to Leicestershire Community Colleges a full-time Assistant Principal, Community, and two other staff with a major commitment to youth and community work certainly make possible a complex diversity of activity beyond the mere provision of comprehensive upper schooling. It is totally inadequate to picture this as embroidery around the hard centre, as ivy on the trunk. It is more deeply interfused.

There is indeed extensive provision for twilight and evening use by the neighbourhood, keeping workshops, theatre and sports hall in heavy employment. The car parks are full every evening in term time, week-ends all day and pretty steadily over the holidays. There are classes and clubs for adult members by day as well. The elderly have their regular afternoon and the infants arrive in their chariots for crèche and clinic. But even all this fails to reveal the connecting links. They are located at dispersed points of interchange between adult world and school student.

Judith's hospital visits exemplify one such interchange because of the way they keyed into her studies in team. Because the team is a small semi-autonomous unit, expeditions are comparatively easy to arrange, involving only the team staff instead of the customary range of departments and the deputy head in charge of timetable. A day visit needs extra team negotiation, but most of the resources in the local community can be tapped in half-day excursions.

The reciprocal penetration by neighbours into the college is qualitatively different from anything that only utilises a detached wing of the building. All the daytime users at Countesthorpe mingle in some degree with the full-time students. And become accepted. During a chat with our weekly class for handicapped people I was told how much they liked seeing our youngsters each week, though at first they had been apprehensive of coming in among adolescents. 'Do you find they hold doors open for you?' I asked. 'Oh yes,' I was told. 'But that's not what we mean.' And with total agreement they told me between them that what they really appreciated, much more than any special attention being given them, was being accepted as normal users of the college in their own right. 'They'll say "Hello", or give you a nod as you go through. They don't pretend we're not there, like most people do. That's what we like.'

It is the blurring of the boundaries between school and non-school, the absence of distinctive school behaviour, ritual, costume, that makes the ebb and flow possible. The other illustrative link I shall choose is that of the adult student who has found her way in to study alongside those who are ten or twenty years younger than her. (They are mostly women, though we have the occasional man who works shifts.)

Countesthorpe has had up to forty such part-time students registered in the course of a year. They nearly all came in for one purpose, most commonly to use the crèche while freed to talk with other mothers, and were then drawn into something more challenging.[7] All of them that I have spoken to wanted to prove to themselves that they could accomplish what they were failed at in their own schooldays, an intellectual study in depth. They start at O-Levels and usually go on to A-Levels. Some use this to enter college or a new job. Most prove something to themselves.

And they prove something to the sixteen- to eighteen-year-olds alongside whom they study. They answer the questions: 'Why are you back in school?' 'What was it like when you were at school?' 'Would you have joined us if school were the same here as where you used to go?' The answers are predictable. Some visitors have found it disconcerting that they could not immediately distinguish between teachers, secondary students, adult students and other callers.[8] Others have found it attractive.

There is no doubt that it is through such interaction that those in their years of secondary schooling may first entertain the notions of lifelong and recurrent education. There is no need for anyone to leave Countesthorpe feeling they have learnt all they can or need to learn from working in a school or college, as distinct from on the shop floor or in the university of life. Let's hope that returning one day, or sending their own children in due course will not be the painful ordeal that so many found it before them.

Conclusions

What may be gathered from the experience of Countesthorpe that may further the development of the open school? I shall complete this chapter with a number of conclusions grouped under ten headings. I have drawn these conclusions from Countesthorpe's established position in the second half of the 1970s, but end with certain lessons that were learnt in the opening years, which in some respects may be past history, but in others, can be applied to any large-scale innovation.

1. On aims
Tim McMullen, Countesthorpe's first Principal drew up a clear set of aims, relating the development of social skills to other forms of learning, and with these attracted a staff with an immediate common purpose. The implementation of the aims was hard and lengthy, but those aims themselves have not been challenged or changed. They have guided all subsequent staff recruitment and curriculum development, which in the absence of agreed aims, could otherwise have been haphazard or at the whim of trends.

Stated goals being various does not mean that 'academic' goals have been abandoned. It may, however, lead to that accusation even from respectable academics in public utterance.[9]

2. Participatory government
Internal government by consensus can be made to work, provided that staff are recruited who wish to operate in that way. Shared decision-making carries shared responsibility, which in turn creates stress. Some teachers prefer to leave both to others. Those who accept the added stress find it more than compensated by the job-satisfaction or professional dignity that it generates.

Conflict is unavoidable, but can be used. Conflict leads through compromise to consensus, and consensus breeds commitment. The Moot principle, requiring consensus rather than simple majority, leads to decisions that are binding.

Students by definition, have a temporary status. They will participate, but need to be informed and encouraged by staff. Staff, unless turnover is high, provide their own continuity: students can lose it. Student sharing in the democracy therefore needs to be consciously sustained. The experience at Countesthorpe is that students participate with a great sense of responsibility, good sense, discernment and discretion.

However, participation, with its committees and working parties is time-consuming. Unless teachers are prepared to give as little time to their families as do Members of Parliament, something else has to be sacrificed. This is most likely to be out-of-hours games and club activity. The replacement value of programmes organised in the extended provision of a community college then assumes additional importance.

3. Relationships and discipline

Discipline, what orders an individual's behaviour and work, needs to be appropriate to the accepted aims. The aim of increased autonomy and responsibility, in school and out, the aim of relating school life more closely to life outside, entail a respect for the law and for other people's rights, rather than a style of coercion and retribution at odds with normal civilian life. This kind of rational discipline can be effective, abandoning corporal punishment or ritual coercion such as enforced 'uniform'. Far from leading to indiscipline, it will, *if persisted in*, lower the level of violence and threat dramatically. Introduced into an established system of strong regulative discipline, it will cause initial turbulence: the teachers will be put to the test. By sticking to their principles in the early period, the Countesthorpe teachers, in refusing to offer violence found in good time that they ceased to be offered any. But it takes nerve.

Genuine respect for teachers will result only from their students perceiving (*a*) competence, (*b*) reciprocity of interest and (*c*) commitment. Given that, formalities are unnecessary and redundant; without that, formalities are a hollow sham. If students are being encouraged simultaneously to acquire the skills of competence and autonomy in their learning, then they will use the ease of access to their teachers responsibly. If they were taught to remain dependent on the teacher, students could become demanding to the point of neurosis. (Again, this is what would be experienced in a transitional phase and it would drive teachers unsure of their aims, or lacking confidence in eventual success, to shut themselves back in their staffroom.)

Under such conditions, the skills of negotiation can be learnt by live interaction.

Teachers unaccustomed to corporate, rational control, will

need to work out their strategies painstakingly. They need to distinguish between leadership and domination,[10] and between authority and authoritarianism. (They also need to learn that, being human, they may sometimes burst out with, 'Look, just do it because I say so.' The real point is whether they can justify their emotional demand when recollected in tranquillity.)

The easy presence of adult students alongside the secondary school students demonstrates (*a*) that the prevailing discipline is acceptable in adult, civilian terms, and (*b*) that, given flexibility of grouping, so that nobody has to spend *all* their study time with the same group, whatever their age, adults and adolescents can mingle and collaborate.

Authority resides in the collective, the Moot and its subdivisions. It is all the more effective for being an authority conferred by those upon whom it is binding. This is democracy, and it works.

4. Curriculum and study

Given all the learning opportunities that a properly endowed comprehensive school can offer, there is no need to chop up the curriculum into little pieces, lessons, and force it by some formula or other into adolescents. Attempts to create a balanced curriculum, regardless of the individual who is to follow it, are bound to fail: rejection will take place somewhere along the line, either by active resistance and consequent disruption, or by passive withdrawal (fight or flight). On the other hand, left to make choices on their own, students will choose in ignorance, or under influence from their peers. The Countesthorpe solution lay in the close guidance that can be given by team-tutors, but only by reuniting the divorced roles of 'pastoral' teacher, who offers *personal* guidance, and 'academic' teacher, who has responsibility for studies in a particular subject. The team-tutor, who spends a major part of each day, possibly half of it, in close contact with the student, is soon in a position to offer personal curriculum guidance. The tutor constructs and reconstructs each student's unique curriculum. Thus, each student's curriculum is balanced for him or her, chosen by informed decisions to which he or she is party, open to renegotiation, but in no sense given or compulsory.

The lesson, in conflict with current trends, is that a compulsory curriculum, or core-curriculum, determined by someone, whether inside school, or outside it locally or nationally, will be ineffective, possibly disastrous, but that there are satisfactory alternatives. However, the alternatives are complex, subtle and non-coercive and therefore of less appeal to the politician wanting a firm, clear message for his public.

5. Student performance

The first lesson is that students will only succeed, in any sense of the word, when they have confidence in the system. Initially, this confidence, or lack of it will reflect parental attitudes and any departure from recognised approaches, however much those approaches may have failed in the past, will arouse parental anxiety and suspicion. This makes the innovative period difficult, since the surest foundation for confidence is evidence of success in those already ahead. The early stumbling-block for many was the absence of streams and options of subject clusters. These had formerly been the outward signs of competent senior school organisation, and lack of them consequently suggested a chaotic mish-mash with no discernible purpose or organisation. Time taught that for the majority of entrants, personalised curriculum choice gave a very fair deal and recognisable success in performance. Individual timetabling bred a high level of motivation, and motivation facilitated development towards autonomy in work.

The evidence for parents of successful performance is most eagerly sought in examinations. A major lesson for teachers lies outside performance in examination, though necessarily related. The individualised studies in team are no mere arrangement for learning English, maths and social studies. The whole aim is to encourage and facilitate enquiry into the unknown, through as wide a variety of modes of learning as possible. Every support is given to students in posing their own problems, not just those given by the teacher, and in drawing their own conclusions, not just reaching what the teacher has predetermined as the right answer. This may be thought to lead to trivial exercises. Sometimes it does. But the lesson is that more often, if teacher and student *share* a line of exploration, whether in maths, local history, drawing, literature or whatever, it can lead to an *intellectual* pursuit, not just with the identifiably bright or 'academic' student, but with students of every ability.[11]

Finally, the evidence, haphazard though it is, points to Countesthorpe students having an increased readiness for the independent study expected of them in higher education. A frequent comment by those who contact us from college or university is that the transition has been relatively easier than their contemporaries from more closely directed sixth forms have found it. It is also significant that their drop-out and failure rate is unusually low.

6. Examinations

Cogent arguments could be advanced for abolishing general examinations at sixteen. However, this would need national action, and any one school has still to operate in a national climate that requires them. If Countesthorpe had originally wanted to avoid public examinations, the staff, on their own principles, would have been bound to respond to the demand that their students would have made for them. As it was, it was agreed to minimise any form of internal examining or testing and to concentrate on study and making the most of the public examining system. The emphasis has been on Mode III examinations, set and marked by the school, moderated externally by the boards. It is far less work for staff to use Mode I, set and marked by the board, and in GCE to use one board. However, advantage may be gained for the students if staff shop around among the boards. Countesthorpe has in this way been able to find the syllabuses that correspond most closely to the studies encouraged in their students.

There is no doubt that the prospect of examination, particularly with the inclusion of assessed course work, provides one source of motivation. However, Countesthorpe cannot be alone in discovering the concomitant disincentives that result in other ways. To take just two, consider the difficulty of taking students *beyond* the requirements of the examination during the final months before papers are set, and, once in sixth form, of persuading students of the value of any activities outside the narrow specialisms of their A-Level courses.

7. Buildings

The design of a school's premises will embody certain social and educational values. These can restrict what the school aims to do, or they can be conducive to them. They don't determine them, but they can help or hinder. Circularity like Countesthorpe's may not appeal to everyone, Western culture having a tradition of rectangularity. Nevertheless, an open school is helped by being horizontal rather than vertical, however prodigal with land this is, and by having many points of entry with similar status.

The architects cannot possibly foresee the detailed utilisation of space that will develop over the years. What is most important is that the spaces should have the maximum adaptability that is compatible with safety and security.

There are those who would say that the major lesson to be drawn from Countesthorpe's architecture is that the fittings (door handles, window frames, ceiling grids, etc.) should have been considerably more robust. Well, yes, that would have helped, especially as the shabby appearance of damaged fittings in the opening year influenced public attitudes so disproportionately. But in the long term, given cost limits, adaptability has proved more important.

8. Staffing, research and development

The staff at Countesthorpe are not superhuman. They are good, but normal teachers. They are unusual in that they subscribe to a common, explicit set of aims. To ensure continuity in this, great pains have to be taken over new appointments. Another difference is that although every member of the staff is a specialist, and most have graduate standing, all have been selected on their readiness to transcend specialism, to understand the whole curriculum, in the way that any Head or deputy elsewhere would be expected to, and within the teams to become involved in the study of other subjects than their own.

These expectations call for in-service education for the teacher. Time for this is never sufficient, but Countesthorpe staff have provided most of their own rethinking sessions. Specialists have laid on seminars after school in programmes of curriculum studies. In some cases the LEA advisers have been useful, sometimes other outside educationists have been invited in. Governors and education committees need to be much freer than the Act at present allows to grant time for periods of internal reappraisal. There ought to be a two-day seminar every year in any developmental school, yet requests for such time in term (absolutely necessary if everyone is expected to attend) have had to be denied to Countesthorpe. In Scandinavia they manage these things better. In Norway all schools are required to spend one day each term on in-service and planning.

When the Principal delegates his authority as extensively as at Countesthorpe, more people spend time on decision-making and administration. This frees him and the deputies to teach. At Countesthorpe, all the teaching staff actually teach, with nobody, including the Principal, on less than a half-timetable. The Principal does not conduct assemblies, leaving this to the teams. He is therefore known in school primarily as a teacher, not as an authority figure. This does not release the Principal from his role as 'external boundaries officer'. The public, as parents, governors, politicians, employers, LEA officers, all require a link-figure to listen and speak on behalf of the college. The time has not come when such a one chosen and put forward by the college itself would be acceptable to that outside world.

The rotation of shared responsibilities, such as serving on committees, and the shared knowledge of administrative details, like finance, may make additional demands of staff, but it has two beneficial effects in particular. It creates greater professional satisfaction, a greater sense of knowing and controlling the factors that determine the conditions of work. Also, it prepares well-experienced candidates for headships and senior posts elsewhere. (Four staff were promoted to headships between 1974 and 1976, and half a dozen have been promoted to deputy headships.) It leaves a problem on the other hand for the younger teacher who may have arrived as a probationer and after anything from three to five years is looking outside for promotion. Most other posts open to him, like a second in department, or a year-head, will leave him well down a hierarchy, excluded from major decisions and cut off from a lot of information. He will have eaten of the Tree of Knowledge and may have to endure a stretch of bitter hunger.

Finally, the large-scale innovations at Countesthorpe have illustrated Tolstoy's thesis that in the heat of battle the generals, let alone the rank and file, cannot know what is happening. Even if there has been less confusion than at Austerlitz and Borodino, it has not always been possible to discern what has been happening. A school in such development needs research officers and skilled observers, not as cold outsiders, but as workers in the same field. Their knowledge of the whole organism must be detailed and intimate. On the few occasions that we have had the benefit of such analysis it has been invaluable. But it should be continuous.

9. Parents and community   2

If the school hasn't the confidence and support of its users (i.e. students and parents), it is doomed:[12] if it has, then it can tell its armchair critics and carpers to push off. The parents and local community of Countesthorpe were initially dismayed by its unfamiliarity and brash confidence. How that support was won is covered to some degree in *The Countesthorpe Experience*. Since then, the clearest reassurance to prospective and new parents has always come from the experienced parents. The elected PTA Committee always sends a few members to preliminary meetings of the strange parents, and their testimony is usually of more effect than anything the staff say.

It is not Countesthorpe's experience alone that parents expect of a school that it should help their children to become skilful, knowledgeable, well behaved and qualified by examination for a suitable employment. Any school knows that.

The ambitious and articulate parent will make those demands clear. The parent who failed at school – and most feel in some degree that they did – may be heard less easily. What they want, when you hear the message, is that if their child is not a front-runner, an A-streamer, he won't be overlooked, but given the opportunity to do the best possible within personal limits. Increasingly steadily with time, has been the volume of response from those parents who have realised that no student at Countesthorpe is ever just a name on the register.

The involvement of parents and the wider local community has been fuller and more effective as a result of the school not erecting traditional ritual barriers. The presence of adults studying alongside school students has had a civilising effect, and has increased the likelihood of the adolescents forming a concept of lifelong or recurrent education.

10. Embarking upon major innovation

Countesthorpe has been studied from this point of view more than once. One immediate proposition is prompted: that acclamation of an innovation will tend to be related inversely to the distance away from it. This 'lighthouse' effect was noted by Robert Norris in the study of Countesthorpe he made for IMTEC.[13]

Local reaction, reflecting more at stake, will be more sceptical and harder to satisfy. The lesson of Countesthorpe's early years, 1970–74, is two-fold. For a major innovation to succeed, the staff must be clear in their aims, committed, resolute and bold. Conversely, they must not take public, and particularly parental support for granted. It has to be won, and it won't be won by information alone. Information is essential, but more important is a long period of patient discussion, free from intimidation. Teachers can be verbally intimidating, talking people into silence and imagining they have convinced them. At the time of Countesthorpe's opening it was necessary for the staff to know and state what they were committed to doing, but they should also have been clearer about which short-term objectives they might have been prepared to modify and then been allowed time to meet a lot of people and do a lot of listening as well as arguing. In that way they might have avoided the crisis of reaction that nearly brought the college to its knees in 1973.

This preparation of attitudes extends to the students embarking upon the innovation, and the teachers of the schools from which they come. However bold the innovation, it is impossible for everything to be different, if only because a school is inescapably a place for learning in. It is therefore critically important that the transition is eased by emphasis being given to features common to both sides of the dividing line of transfer rather than concentrating the preparation on the novelties. Staff at the feeder schools will be professionally slighted if their work is devalued, and much will depend for years to come on their support rather than their hostility.

One clear lesson for the local authorities is that no school, let alone an innovatory school, should be allowed to open with any boys or girls in their last year of schooling. Adjustment in that time is impossible, and for any with resentments against school there is an invitation to retaliate against the system before it can recognise and deal with them.

A further point to add is that parents and teachers are voters. If more than a few of them are allowed to become disgruntled, their cause in a democracy will be taken up by their representatives. Unfortunately, there is political advantage to be gained by championing the dissatisfied citizen, especially if teachers or 'bureaucrats' can be stigmatised as the villains, and the school that has carried its innovations beyond public tolerance will become a political shuttlecock. This hurts staff and students alike. The moral is that while rash innovators should avoid pushing their luck at the expense of their charges, so by the same token, politicians should deny themselves the glory of espousing the cause of a lone protester merely out to exploit public attention.

It is almost unavoidable that radical innovation will produce external reaction and pressure to revert and conform. This may come from within the profession as well as from parents, politicians, the press and officers of the local administration. The pressure may take many forms, hard and soft. The British have a genius for alternating the velvet glove and the mailed fist. For the innovators, their fate turns on how nicely they can judge the balancing point between sweating it out in solid unity and compromising on principle. Countesthorpe won through, with supporters, acknowledged and unacknowledged, but others have been forced to retreat. It is all a battle for confidence.

Finally it must be proclaimed that the major lesson that Countesthorpe gives is that it has happened at all and survived to span the 1970s. There have been enormous vested interests to see that it did not start or survive, there were regiments of Jeremiahs who said it couldn't work; traducers have welcomed derogatory stories about it to amplify, true or false. To some it has remained a threat to accepted styles and values in education: to others it has embodied a hope of something radically different that will make sense of schooling in the future. Other radical departures within the maintained system have faltered or failed under the weight of opposition. Even if, for one reason or another, Countesthorpe should now fade into stagnation or revert to some more familiar form, even if it is remembered only as a ten-year operation, it will have been enough. It will have proved its point and left its mark indelibly on the unfolding story of public education.

Notes

1. A short bibliography of references to and articles on Countesthorpe College:
   Michael Armstrong, 'Reconstructing knowledge: an example', *Forum for the Discussion of New Trends in Education*, 17, No. 2, Spring 1975;
   Pat D'Arcy, et al., *Keeping Options Open*, Schools Council and University of London Institute of Education, 1974;
   John Macbeath (ed.), *A Question of Schooling*, Hodder and Stoughton, 1976;
   Stewart Mason (ed.), *In Our Experience*, Longman, 1970;
   R. S. Peters, (ed.) *The Role of the Head*, Routledge and Kegan Paul, 1977;
   William Prescott, *Portrait of Countesthorpe College*, Case Study 5.E203, The Open University, 1976;
   B. Simon, and Caroline Benn, *Half Way There*, Penguin, 2nd edn, 1972; Phillip Taylor, and Jack Walton, (eds) *Curriculum, Research, Innovation and Change*, Ward Lock Educational, 1973;
   B. Turner, (ed.), *Discipline in Schools*, Ward Lock Educational, 1973;

J. F. Watts, (ed.), *The Countesthorpe Experience*, Allen and Unwin, 1977;
J. F. Watts, *Teaching*, David and Charles, 1974.

2. See S. Mason, *In our Experience*, Longman, 1970.
3. Subversive acts in an institution may often be expressed in reaction to architecture, as in climbing through windows, going up a 'down-staircase', or traversing the corridor marked 'Private'.
4. At times it has met fortnightly, alternating with a smaller meeting of its executive, but the effect is still to clear business weekly.
5. J. F. Watts, 'The role of the head in participatory government'. Originally in R. S. Peters (ed.), *The Role of the Head*, Routledge and Kegan Paul, 1976. Reprinted in J. Watts (ed.) *The Countesthorpe Experience*.
6. *The Countesthorpe Experience*, Ch. 4.
7. An article by Christine English, 'I only came for the crèche', in *The Countesthorpe Experience*, Ch. 12.
8. Mr John Farr, MP, reported in the *Leicester Mercury* 31 Mar. 1973.
9. G. Bantock, 'A question of quality' a paper published in *A Question of Schooling*, J. E. C. MacBeath (ed.), Hodder and Stoughton, 1976, with a reply in the same volume by John Watts, 'Creative conflict'; and more directly by Michael Armstrong in *The Countesthorpe Experience*, Ch. 20, an exchange of letters between Armstrong and Bantock.
10. Cf. D. Cooper, *Psychiatry and Anti-psychiatry*, Tavistock Publications, 1967; Poladin edn, 1970, quoted in Ch. 6, p. 82.
11. A fuller study of this central issue, pursued at Countesthorpe, would entail reading several articles by Michael Armstrong, but principally, 'Reconstructing knowledge: an example', Ch. 8 of *The Countesthorpe Experience*, originally published in *Forum for the Discussion of New Trends in Education*, 17, No. 2, Spring 1975.
12. It has been pointed out to me that my inclusion of parents as 'users' at this point conflicts with an earlier use of the term seeming to imply students and teachers only. I can only say that this reflects the very ambivalent position of parents of children in the 14–19 age range. When their children are fourteen, parents may expect some right and obligation of control and direction: by nineteen they will, if wise, have learnt to relinquish both. Thus in so far as they are 'users', parents have a wasting status.
13. R. Norris, 'Countesthorpe in an international context', in *The Countesthorpe Experience*, Ch. 22. IMTEC (International Management Training for Educational Change) formerly an offshoot of CERI/DECD is directed from Oslo by Per Dalin.

10 Persons not products: a new covenant

If we are any closer, at the end of this book, to the concept of an open school, it is worth attempting answers to two questions: 'What will it be like to work in one?' 'What would be learnt there?' The first question calls for a summary of all that has gone so far in terms of relationships. The second returns us to curriculum.

The key to both of them is to be found in the mutual attitudes of teachers and students. My argument has been that in spite of all kinds of novelties in school, the basic element of coercion has remained unaltered – that when it comes down to it, what teachers are seen as being there for is to tell their students what to do and see that they do it. There is much support within society for this attitude. What I am calling for is a radical change in this basic attitude, for a replacement of coercion by contract. In fact, a new contract, or covenant, needs to be drawn up to give clarity and vigour to the working agreement that might be made between reasonable, consenting people, in contrast to a continuous confrontation between warring tribes. A little later in this chapter I shall present such a draft covenant.

Concerning curriculum, there may be a world of difference between what any authority decrees should be taught and what in fact is learnt. In spite of considerable recent shift of emphasis in learning theory from what the teacher teaches to what the learner learns, a pious expectation still dominates educational politics that what is learnt can be determined by a directed curriculum. The theory runs as follows: we can work out what they need to know, we can draw this up as the core-curriculum (add what frills you like), we can make this compulsory in all schools, and, Bingo! they'll all know it. Or if they don't it must be because the teachers lack the good old-fashioned backbone to discipline them into learning their lessons. If this book has served any purpose, it will have been to add weight to the argument that such a theory is mistaken, not only because in the name of humanity that *ought* not to be the approach, but because it just cannot work in practice. A compulsory curriculum is impossible if looked at in terms, not of what is taught, but of what is learnt.

All that the curriculum can do is present a range of areas of learning on offer to the student. The curriculum may facilitate or it may restrict the learning opportunities, but it can never determine them. All too often a school's curriculum is essentially the sum of its examination syllabuses, with little or no regard for whether the content of those syllabuses relates particularly to the demands of the occupations they are meant to give qualification for, or whether they add up to any preparation for living in the decades ahead.

However, with the caveat that curriculum can offer but not determine, there are certain elements that seem to have little or no place as yet in the common run of secondary school curricula, but which, on the arguments I have already advanced in earlier chapters, ought to be on offer. In a short list of these, I would include the following:

1. the means of enlarging understanding of the self, of others and the relationships between self and others;
2. the means of understanding and engaging with local communities;
3. the means of understanding political operations so as to appreciate what is happening to oneself politically and the means of taking democratic action;
4. the means of interpreting the mass-media and direct communications, so as to distinguish information from opinion; to understand the nature of evidence and the nature of prejudice;
5. the means of understanding the interdependence of all peoples of the world, politically, economically and ecologically;
6. the means of distinguishing hypothesis from dogma, in science, politics and religion;
7. the means of finding how to live to the fullest within a clear

understanding of our limits, spiritual, emotional, economic and technological, both personally and globally.

It might be argued that all this is covered by the conventional studies in the school curriculum – history, geography, language, literature, religion, science, music, physical education, art and craft. What more do we want? Well, it *could* all be introduced within those subjects: my complaint is that it *isn't*. It is just possible that the reformed curriculum could grow under the clothing of the old terminology. The Countesthorpe experience was that too drastic a change in the *appearance* of things can shake confidence and thus obstruct the reform, and that new terms (like IG for study of Individuals and Groups) did not help the restructuring of social studies intended. What names we use becomes a pragmatic question, to be answered in individual situations. The real issue is what will actually be going on. You can rename History as 'Political Studies', or Geography as 'The Individual and the Environment', but if what happens in class is still learning dates of famous Acts of Parliament and tracing maps, then 'what's in a name?'

The essential difference is not in the name but in the nature of the studies open to students, and that stems from basic attitudes on the part of the teachers. In the end no one will determine what is learnt other than the teacher and students between them at the interface. Obviously, the resources available and the skills brought to bear on both sides of that interface will have immense importance, but even these will not determine the outcome. With the same resources available, totally different outcomes will result from teachers operating from different basic assumptions.

The curriculum opportunities I have listed above will have little or no long-term effectiveness if merely translated into pre-packaged knowledge to be got into kids. You cannot *instruct* the adolescent in self-knowledge or political deception or social interaction, any more than you can teach swimming from charts, or spot-welding from dictated notes: those techniques have a place in the teacher's repertoire, but essentially he has to get his students out of their desks *doing* these things. Ultimately, we learn about other people by interacting with them. And you cannot be coerced into doing these things. Encouragement, praise, exposure to the need for embarking upon them, are all necessary. Nobody enjoys being ignorant, it is contrary to human nature: the test of the true teacher is to identify an area of significant ignorance and to convince his students that it is significant to *them*. (One is reminded of the Harlem boy who when asked by his teacher how many legs a grasshopper has, replied, 'Man, I sure wish I had your problems'.)[1]

So I am asking for these curriculum elements to be built into the life of the school, not just worked into the timetable of existing subjects. But they must be included consciously and the student made conscious of them. Liam Hudson has warned, in *The Cult of the Fact*, that not only will the imparting of facts remain sterile, but that the transmitted assumptions carry their own dangers.

> . . . every generation of students is susceptible to its teachers' presuppositions, and . . . these presuppositions are potent just to the extent that they are unspoken. It is assumptions, prejudices and implicit metaphors that are the true burden of what passes between teacher and taught. Facts, skills, details are in comparison ephemeral, in sciences especially, but in the arts as well. They are also identifiable – and rejectable. What the teacher spells out the pupil can question. What he assumes, especially from a position of unchallenged legitimacy, his pupils will tend to swallow whole and unawares.[2]

Thus every school has its hidden curriculum, and needs to ask itself how, and how often, it should be exposed and scrutinised.

Liam Hudson's point also reveals the difficulty of avoiding indoctrination. Eliminating indoctrination from the curriculum is like trying to exterminate rats on a farm. As fast as you get rid of them in one barn, they start breeding in another: you poison them with wolfram and a resistant strain appears. A school may scrupulously purge its printed resources of dogmatic assertions about imperialism, communism, racism, sexism, and any other -isms, only to find that the most potent indoctrination takes place through the unstated assumptions of the teacher. What can one do? Only, I believe, lay oneself open as a teacher to constant invited challenge, and announce the possibility of the very framework of the studies concerned being fallible. Hudson is also pertinent in identifying the problem: ·

> If a teacher successfully transmits his own beliefs about the limits of legitimate enquiry he is, de facto, an indoctrinator. Yet it is a condition of productive brain-work that one is committed to a discipline of some sort. So, it would seem that the teacher who leaves his students' minds open, in a state of promiscuous athleticism, is scarcely a teacher at all. His proper function, in other words, must be an ambiguous one.[3]

The only solution to this dilemma would seem to be one of the teacher displaying a vigorous fallibilism – vigorous enough to inspire his students into activity, fallible enough to let them know that his own hypotheses and conclusions are open to modification or replacement.

Such an approach implies to the student that the teacher is also a learner, that the problems to which the student addresses himself are capable of yielding answers in which the teacher has an interest. It implies that 'the teacher' may learn from 'the student'. Such a reversal of roles is unthinkable in a basically authoritarian system, and its suggestion is a dangerous threat. There can be no half-measures about this. There cannot be a peaceful co-existence of reciprocal interests in the classroom and imposed authority in the corridors. For such an attitude to learning to prevail, the whole school must be an expression of reciprocal interest, of mutual respect between teachers and students.

It has always been possible that the good teacher would learn with or from his students. In our time it has become imperative that he should. Whatever the remaining strength of our traditions, both academic and social, we are experiencing more intensely than at any time in recorded history, a rate and quality of change that causes reference to the past for guidance to be of rapidly decreasing helpfulness. This is a bitter pill for the elders to swallow. Traditionally, wisdom has resided in the tribal elders, and in my own belief, on fundamental, universal truths, probably still does. But the advice of the middle-aged and elderly was not sought so much on fundamental truths as on day-to-day practical guidance, the know-how of getting the world's work done. It is this that has changed so disconcertingly. It is little use complaining about declining respect for the older generation. They just haven't got so much to offer and they have more to answer for in the present condition of mankind than is comfortable.

In an analysis of this upheaval, Margaret Mead describes it as a shift from a post-figurative culture, where the past determines the present, to one of pre-figurative culture, which is determined by the future and its young. This presents a painful moral problem to which she offers this hope: 'We must create new models for adults who can teach their children not what to learn, but how to learn and not what they should be committed to, but the value of commitment.'[4]

If this need is so urgent, why is it not being attended to in any concerted way in schools? Largely because of the inertia of traditional styles. That something can be done to move in the direction Margaret Mead was advocating has been demonstrated at Countesthorpe. But the hazards have also been shown. It is not a reform that can be effected by bureaucratic means. It needs careful organisation, but the organisation must be enabling, in the way that the administration of a good local education authority will enable. It needs organisation, but it is not *about* organisation. It is about allowing and assisting people to become themselves and relate to each other as people, not just as means to material ends.

This is difficult because the most obvious models of organisation are those found in industry. Schools have suffered, and continue to suffer terrible penalties for accepting these inappropriate models. Especially at a time of national financial and industrial crisis, these models are thrust upon Heads and teachers. The pressure comes from well-intentioned, and not so well-intentioned, governors and employers, and alas, from colleagues who have jumped upon the 'management' band-wagon. The models are inappropriate because they have been designed with products and production in mind. They relate to the processing of raw material into marketable goods. Surrounding the process of production are the business concepts of cost-effectiveness, output norms, quality control, competitive sales and so on. All this can be translated into terms of school if it is once granted that children are our raw material, to be processed into a marketable product. It is a seductive line of thought, and many have adopted it. It should be exposed and denounced as dehumanising, reducing humans to things, and anathema to education and life, something nobody in their right mind would apply to their own child and ought not to apply to anyone else's children.

The alternative model is one organised around caring communities. The school itself can be a unit in which mutual care is the keynote of all activity. How can this be realised in a large school? Nobody can *care* in any true sense of the word for 1,000 others: you can hardly know their names. In the sense of being concerned about what is happening to them, attending sensitively to the welfare of those found to be in need, a Head may be said to 'care' for his students, but he cannot 'care' for each one as one might a son or daughter: there are just too many. You can only know, and therefore care for, practically, about 200 others.

Does this mean we must apply Schumacher's dictum 'small is beautiful' literally, and keep schools down in size? If so, what becomes of the curriculum organised for 1,000? The answer lies in the formation of sub-units, not just for some loose 'pastoral' guidance with limited contact, but as mini-schools with a high degree of autonomy and long regular working periods committing the student and teacher members to close contact. Given the security and intimacy of such sub-units, if each one does not rise much above 200, the problem of total size of school all but disappears. At least, the limit on size becomes organisational, and is no longer social.

The sub-school solution has operated successfully in places as far apart as Countesthorpe and Auckland. The New Zealand

Department of Education in 1975 adopted in principle the plan for schools based on sub-units with just such a function as the Countesthorpe teams, though with a somewhat larger unit membership. In tribute to the Maori origin of the concept, the units are given their name for the extended family, *whanau*. The first *whanau* unit was added on to Penrose High School, Auckland, and opened in 1977. Schools based entirely on *whanaus* are under construction.[5] Not far away, in Melbourne, Australia, Huntingdale Technical School has evolved a sub-school system which was the basis of the design for their new buildings when they opened in 1979. In both these instances, the development was seen as neither architectural nor administrative in its origin, but as social and educational.[6]

In various ways, then, practical working answers *have been found* to the problem of making school, while still a public institution, into a caring community of learning, instead of a factory for examinations or a sorting house for employment in an industrial society. But in each case there has been no mere tinkering. A revolution of aims and methods has been entailed. R. S. Peters has shrewdly remarked, 'The crucial question to ask, when men wax enthusiastic of their aims, is what procedures are to be adopted in order to implement them.'[7] For the cold-shower effect, this is fair play. However, the case I have made will pass this test. It has been tried in practice, right round the world, and found to work.

Looking at colleges that have operated for enough years to prove their points, as far apart as Leicestershire, England and Melbourne, Victoria, we can ask what sort of working agreement between teachers and students has made it possible. It must be an agreement between all parties, including parents and the local community. In that sense, it is a covenant, 'a mutual agreement between two or more persons to do or refrain from doing certain acts'.[8] There must have been a million 'school rules' drawn up, none with the consent of those upon whom they were meant to be binding (in contrast to the laws of a democracy). For a change, I offer here a basis for contract, a draft covenant, for all those in upper secondary schooling.

A Covenant for upper secondary schools, whereby it is granted

A. to all students that they

1. will have full access to all the resources for learning both in and out of school, and regardless of which school they attend;
2. will have maximum access to the teachers they may learn from, regardless of whether or not what they want to learn is examinable;
3. will have maximum choice of whom they wish to work with;
4. will have choice of what they want to study;
5. will be assured of facilities for work and study free from disruption;
6. will be given every encouragement to develop their own style of work and take responsibility for organising their own patterns of learning and leisure;
7. will have full professional encouragement, instruction, guidance and assessment, not only by formal examination but by assessment of performance over a period or course;
8. will be free from examinations whose necessity is not demonstrable;
9. will be encouraged in self-assessment;
10. will be respected by teachers for what they *are*, not what they *will be*, or *will produce*; that they will be regarded as persons, not products;
11. will be free to express honest emotions, to discover who they are;
12. will be free from the restrictive labelling of IQ or other artificial limiting descriptions of global ability, such as streaming produces;
13. will be free from the threat of corporal punishment and other forms of retribution and humiliation;
14. will be free to dress as they choose;
15. will be free to express and argue points of view or political conviction;

16. will be free to assemble and express collective points of view;
17. will be free to comment, critically and constructively, on their teachers;
18. will be encouraged to play an active part in the formulation of the school's aims and the planning of its curriculum, participating with their teachers, and with representation on the governing body;
19. will be protected from political or religious indoctrination;
20. will be enabled to work and live in collaboration with rather than in competition with other;

B. to all teachers that they

1. will have maximum opportunity to participate in the formulation of aims, policy-making and organisation of the school, thus collectively determining, with their students, the internal conditions of work;
2. may expect that all members of the teaching staff teach;
3. will have means of easy communication with everyone else on staff;
4. will be given opportunities and encouraged to develop their skills, teaching, social and managerial, within the organisation of the school;
5. will have a right of appeal to their colleagues against decisions taken by anyone else or other groups on staff;
6. may expect students and teachers to show mutual respect for each other;
7. will be allowed time at regular intervals to make collective and unhurried reappraisals of aims and progress;
8. may feel encouraged to send their own children to the school where they teach, free of anxiety or embarrassment;
9. will be given opportunity to exchange visits (*a*) with teachers in other schools, (*b*) with people working in other occupations;
10. will have a large say in the selection of fellow teachers and the Head or Principal;

C. to all parents that they

1. will become partners with their sons and daughters, and their teachers in designing the curriculum and in the choices made within it;
2. will be kept regularly informed about the life of the school and the performance of their own children in particular;
3. will be given easy access to the Head and other teachers, with the right to call for *ad hoc* reports;
4. will have a right to see any other reports relating to them and their children;
5. will be welcome, at reasonable intervals, not just at 'open days', to see the school at normal work;
6. will be informed of career prospects and job openings and be drawn into consultation at appropriate times;
7. will be able to elect their representatives on the board of governors, be kept informed by them and have a right to a hearing by the board of governors;
8. will be free from any directive or pressure from school over what their children shall wear, apart from protective clothing where there is danger to health or safety;
9. will have their children protected at school from interference, assault, humiliation or indoctrination whether by other students, teachers or other users of the school;
10. will be enabled, without restrictive practice, to give to the school whatever help the teachers and students would welcome.

Such a covenant provides checks and balances which make it dangerous to pick out individual clauses from the context of the others. For example, to take separately the students' rights to assemble and express collectively political views (15 and 16) would be hopelessly divisive, if not volcanic, in a school where there was no continuous participation of students and teachers in the decision-making. Banner-waving and slogan-chanting are likely to be manifestations of long-denied opportunities for effective expression and action, signs of desperation (or else mere play-acting). Where students assume a right of action in a school that has not prepared for it, or where the other clauses of this covenant, or most of them, have not been adopted, there will be conflict, possibly destructive. Taken in conjunction with the rest of the covenant, the two clauses are hardly contentious at all. Where the rights of assembly and expression can be taken for granted, they are unlikely to prove explosive, because a legal assembly or expression is not used to demonstrate something in itself, being merely a means to an end, to getting things done.

I am sceptical of overnight transformations in any walk of life, and would be very worried about any groups, parents, students or teachers, nailing my covenant on the door. Reform may take leaps and bounds, rather than get far by creeping, but the leaps need to be prepared and the bounds made in full daylight. The covenant may be a target, and individuals and groups must work out their own strategies for reaching it according to their local circumstances, their own strengths and weaknesses, their resources and their degree of unanimity and resolution. Incautious innovation may produce nothing but destructive reaction. This I have called the Actaeon effect.

Actaeon, it may be remembered, was a king who loved hunting deer. One day, following his hounds in full scent, he blundered into a forest glade and surprised the goddess Diana herself, bathing naked with her attendant nymphs at a spring. Fascinated by her dazzling beauty, he stayed gazing until he was seen by the goddess. Outraged by his audacity, she had him transformed on the spot into a stag. And then, in spite of his attempts to cry out in protest and identify himself, he was hunted down by his own hounds and torn to pieces.

Diana was goddess of the hunt and also of the moon. The hunter after innovation must take care then, that he does not become moonstruck, overwhelmed by the vision of reformation in its radiant nakedness. The problem for the innovator is that he must run just so far ahead to give a lead to those that will follow him, but not to outstrip them to the point where he may no longer be recognisable, lest his followers become his pursuers and hunt him down. Credibility has to be maintained, and the pace set accordingly.

What I am asking for with this covenant can be constructed, given a basic premise that each student is already a person, not just a potential, and never a product. The emphasis has of late been upon improved management. Now we ought not to despise efficient administration: it makes things possible which muddle and mess prevent or retard. The danger is that management and efficiency are so easily identified with improved *productivity*, elimination of wasted time, space and serendipity. But this is not what education is about.

Education is, as much as anything, about enabling people to realise who they are, to recognise what potential they have within themselves and to reach the means of fulfilling it. As often as not, the teacher then has, above all, to avoid interrupting the process. I tend to agree with Bill Romey's 'Ashlad hypothesis'. Drawing on the Norwegian legend of the Ashlad, a male Cinderella, who is left behind but always makes good, Romey declares 'a relaxed, intuitive, spontaneous, gentle, aware, and generous approach to problems may lead to a solution before an institutionalised, rigid, formalistic, procedurally-oriented approach'. He also says, 'the less we interfere with people and their unique ways of exploring within a rich environment encompassing all aspects of society, the more they may grow in ways consonant with their own potential'.[9]

Our education has its roots in pious and joyless industry where children grinding away in school were only one step removed from children grinding away in employment, even, within living memory, doing both on alternate days. Our social consciousness has not yet made the adjustments of the work-ethic that are becoming inescapable. As it does, it may, hopefully, recognise that Western culture is monstrously over-productive and wasteful of resources. We squander our physical resources and neglect our creativity. Sooner or later, we shall be forced to accept that all our necessary production will be carried out by fewer people with less effort, and that education must be geared, not to joyless productivity, but to autonomous creativity. We just are hopelessly unprepared as yet for the enforced leisure to come. We are dominated by spectator sports and mechanical time-filling, fruit machines and bingo. We must avoid the nostalgia of basket-weaving and Morris dancing and begin to evolve creative communities of new kinds. We may as yet hardly begin to envisage them. They will be shaped by our children and grandchildren as they grow up, but only if they have been allowed to dabble in the ashes.

When the Swedish government, seeking a reform of its educational system in 1962 asked an advisory team for a basis upon which to construct all schooling, they were given the reply, '*Sang och saga, lek och poesi*'. 'Song and story, play and poetry.' Their parliament had the wisdom to accept it.

Epilogue

This book has been an appeal for an alternative approach to schooling within the existing framework of compulsory education, maintained by the public system. It is not crying for the moon, nor calling for drastic and expensive reorganisation. It is urging changes in attitude.

What is being asked for has been attempted in isolated instances. Some of the chronicled achievements have been short-lived: others, like that of Terry O'Neill, lasted for decades.[10] The evidence is enough to show what can be done with the necessary will. It is also enough to reveal the pattern of difficulties that will be encountered in any alternative development of the open variety.

Since finishing this book, I have had the opportunity to spend some time looking at the work of Tony Delves and his staff at Huntingdale Technical School in Melbourne, to visit Morialta High School in Adelaide, and to revisit Penrose High School in Auckland, NZ, where their first *whanau* is operational. I have also, belatedly, been able to read studies of the Metro High School of Chicago. From all of this, I am more than ever convinced of the need for alternatives within the system that will approach more closely the ideal of the open school. And I am more than ever convinced that it can be done.

Moreover, there is now a sufficient body of documented experience from those who have ventured in these directions to assist the next generation of innovators in planning more workable strategies and to arm them against the inevitable flak. We do not need, in fact we cannot afford, to reinvent the wheel before the wagons can roll. But if the 'alternative' movement is to be more than a fringe manifestation, if it is to provide a steady working reality, then those engaged in organising it must start to learn from what has already been undertaken, the successes and the failures.

This growing corpus of experience may be regarded, paradoxically, as a fresh tradition. It is an 'alternative' tradition, and by working within it, by advancing it, we may be able to move towards an open school with the least waste of time and human spirit. The task is urgent.

John Watts
Countesthorpe, December, 1978

Notes

1. Quoted in N. Postgate, and C. Weingartner, *Teaching as a Subversive Activity*, Dell Publishing Co. Inc, New York, 1969; Penguin, 1971.
2. L. Hudson, *The Cult of the Fact*, Jonathan Cape, 1972, p. 43.
3. Ibid., p. 98.
4. M. Mead, *Culture and Commitment*, Bodley Head, 1970.
5. *Secondary Schools for Tomorrow – A New Approach to Design and Construction*, NZ Department of Education, 1975.
6. Tony Delves, *Huntingdale – Five Years Later*, Dialogue, 10, No. 3, Dec. 1976.
7. R. S. Peters, *Authority, Responsibility and Education*, Allen and Unwin, 1960.
8. *Shorter Oxford English Dictionary*.
9. Bill Romey, *Consciousness and Creativity: Transcending Science, Humanities and the Arts*, New York, The Ashlad Press, 1975.
10. Gerard Holmes, *The Idiot Teacher*, Faber, 1952. Re-issued with preface by John Watts, Spokesman Press, 1977.

Select bibliography

ABERCROMBIE, L., *The Anatomy of Judgement*, Penguin, 1969.
ASHBY, B. K., *Joseph Ashby of Tysoe 1859–1919*. CUP, 1961; Merlin Press, 1974.
BARNES, D., *From Communication to Curriculum*, Penguin, 1976.
BARNES, D. et al, *Language, the Learner and the School*, Penguin, 1971.
BECHER, T. and MACLURE, S., *The Politics of Curriculum Change*, Hutchinson, 1978.
BENN, C. and SIMON, B., *Halfway There* (2nd edn), Penguin, 1972.
BERNSTEIN, B., 'Open school, open society?', *New Society*, 14 Sept. 1967.
BERNSTEIN, B., ELVIN, H. and PETERS, R. S., Ritual in Education *Philosophical Transactions of the Royal Society of London* (B), 1966 251 (772), 429–36.
BLYTHE, RONALD, *Akenfield*, Allen Lane, 1969.
BOARD OF EDUCATION, *The Education of the Adolescent* (The Hadow Report), HMSO, 1926.
Report of the Consultative Committee on the Primary School (The Hadow Report), HMSO, 1931.
Report of the Consultative Committee on Secondary Education (The Spens Report), HMSO, 1938.
Curriculum and Examinations in Secondary Schools (The Norwood Report), HMSO, 1943.
BRITTON, J., *Language and Learing*, Allen Lane; Penguin, 1971.
BRITTON, J. et al., *The Development of Writing Abilities 11–18*, Schools Council 1974.
BULLOCK, A., *A Language for Life* (The Bullock Report) HMSO, 1975.
CHRISTIE, Nils, *If the School Wasn't There*, Oslo, University Press.
COOPER, D., *Psychiatry and Antipsychiatry*. Tavistock Publications, 1967.
COX, C. B. and DYSON, A. E. (eds), *Fight for Education, A Black Paper*, Critical Quarterly Society, 1969.
DALIN, PER, *Strategies for Innovation in Education*, Paris, OECD, 1972.
DEPARTMENT OF EDUCATION AND SCIENCE, *Teacher Education and Training: a report by a committee of enquiry* (The James Report), HMSO, 1972.
DEWEY, J., *The School and Society*, University of Chicago Press, 1900.
DICKENS, C., *Hard Times*, 1854.
DOUGLAS, J. W., ROSS, J. M. and SIMPSON, H. R., *All Our Future, A Longitudinal Study of Secondary Education*, Peter Davies, 1968.
FOGELMAN, K. (ed.), *Britain's Sixteen-year-olds*, National Children's Bureau, 1976.

FREIRE, P., *Pedagogy of the Oppressed*, Penguin, 1972.
FROMM, E., *Fear of Freedom*, Routledge and Kegan Paul, 1942.
FROMM, E., *The Sane Society*, Routledge and Kegan Paul, 1956.
GARNETT, EMMELINE, *Area Resource Centre: An Experiment*, Edward Arnold, 1972.
GOFFMAN, E., *Asylums*, Anchor Books, 1961; Penguin, 1968.
GRIFFIN, D., *Slow Learners*, Woburn Press, 1978.
HEAD, D. (ed.), *Free Way to Learning*, Penguin, 1974.
HOLLY, D. (ed.), *Education or Domination?*, Arrow Books, 1974.
HOLLY, D., *Society Schools and Humanity*, MacGibbon and Kee, 1971.
HOLMES, GERARD, *The Idiot Teacher*, Faber, 1952. Reissued with preface by John Watts, Spokesman Press, 1977.
HOLT, J., *How Children Fail*, Dell Publishing Co., 1964.
HUDSON, L., *The Cult of the Fact*, Jonathan Cape, 1972.
ILLICH, I. D., *Deschooling Society*, Calder and Boyars, 1971.
JACKSON, B. *Streaming: An Education System in Miniature*, Routledge and Kegan Paul, 1964.
JACKSON, B. and MARSDEN, D., *Education and the Working Class*, Routledge and Kegan Paul, 1962.
JONES, PAULINE, *Community Education in Practice – A Review*, The Social Evaluation Unit, Oxford University Press, 1978.
LANGER, SUZANNE, *Philosophy in a New Key*, Cambridge, Mass., Harvard University Press, 1942.
MACBEATH, J. (ed.), *A Question of Schooling*, Hodder and Stoughton, 1976.
MARTIN, N. et al., *Writing and Learning Across the Curriculum*, Ward Lock Educational, 1976.
MASON, S. (ed.), *In our Experience*, Longman, 1970.
MEAD, M., *Culture and Commitment*, Bodley Head, 1970.
MEDAWAR, P., *The Art of the Soluble*, Penguin, 1969.
MOORE, D. R. et al., 'Strengthening alternative high schools', *Harvard Educational Revue*, vol. 42 no. 3, Aug. 1972.
MORRELL, D., 'Happiness is not a meal ticket', *The Times Educational Supplement*, 19 Dec. 1969.
NEWELL, P., *A Last Resort*, Penguin, 1972.
NEWSOM, J., *Half our Future* (The Newsom Report) HMSO, 1963.
PEDLEY, R., *The Comprehensive School*, Penguin, 2nd edn, 1969.
PETERS, R. S. *Authority, Responsibility and Education*, Allen and Unwin, 1960.
PETERS, R. S. (ed.), *The Role of the Head*, Routledge, 1976.
POPPER, K., *The Open Society and Its Enemies*, Routledge and Kegan Paul, 1945.
POSTER, C., *The School and the Community*, Macmillan, 1971.
POSTGATE, N. and WEINGARTNER, C., *Teaching as a Subversive Activity*, 1969.
PRINGLE, MIA KELLMER, *The Roots of Violence and Vandalism*, National Children's Bureau, 1973.
REE, H., *Educator Extraordinary: the Life and Achievement of Henry Morris*, Longman, 1973.
RUBINSTEIN, D. and SIMON, B., *The Evolution of the Comprehensive*

School 1926–72, Routledge and Kegan Paul, 2nd edn, 1973.

SARASON, S. B., *The Culture of the School and the Problem of Change*, Allyn and Bacon, 1971.

SCHUMACHER, E. F., *Small is Beautiful*, Blond and Briggs, 1973.

SOMERSET, C., *Littledene: Patterns of Change*, NZ Department of Education.

TAYLOR, W., *Society and the Education of Teachers*, Faber, 1969.

TAYLOR, L., *Resources for Learning*, Penguin, 1971.

TAYLOR, P. and WALTON, J. (eds), *Curriculum Research, Innovation and Change*, Ward Lock Educational, 1973.

TOFFLER, A., *Future Shock*, Random House, 1970.

TURNER, B. (ed.), *Discipline in Schools*, Ward Lock Educational, 1975.

VYGOTSKY, L. S., *Thought and Language*, Cambridge, Mass., MIT Press, 1962.

WATTS, J. F., *Teaching*, David and Charles, 1974.

WATTS, J. F., *The Countesthorpe Experience*, Allen and Unwin, 1977.

WRIGHT, N., *Progress in Education*, Croom Helm, 1977.

YOUNG, M. F. D. (ed.), *Knowledge and Control*, Collier-Macmillan, 1972

Index